NETWORK
Your Way to
SUCCESS

About the Author

John Timperley is the author of *Barefoot on Broken Glass*, the five secrets of success in a massively changing business world. Formerly Managing Director of an international public relations consultancy, he is now a Marketing Director with the world's largest professional services firm, PricewaterhouseCoopers. A regular speaker and presenter on business development issues, he has created, and delivers, networking training programmes for both clients and staff.

John has won several awards for his marketing campaigns in both the private and the public sectors, including the prestigious Professional Marketing International Award and an Institute of Public Relations 'Sword of Excellence'. He lives in the Lancashire village of Wardle with his wife Joanne and three daughters, Melissa, Jessica and Hannah.

NETWORK
Your Way to
SUCCESS

Discover the Secrets
of the World's Top
Connectors

JOHN TIMPERLEY

PIATKUS

Copyright © 2002 by John Timperley

First published in 2002 by
Judy Piatkus (Publishers) Limited
5 Windmill Street
London W1T 2JA
e-mail: info@piatkus.co.uk

The moral rights of the author have been asserted

A catalogue record for this book is available from the British Library

ISBN 0–7499–2283-4

This book has been printed on paper manufactured with respect for the environment using wood from managed sustainable resources

Text design by Paul Saunders
Copy editing by Lizzie Hutchins

Typeset by Action Publishing Technology Ltd, Gloucester
Printed and bound in Great Britain by
The Bath Press, Bath, Somerset

Dedication

To my wife Joanne and our three daughters, Melissa, Jessica and Hannah.

I said I wouldn't write another one, but I have! At the heart of this book is the message that you have to give first in order to receive. You have made sacrifices to give me the time and support I needed to capture my thoughts to benefit others. Now it's my turn to repay you in full – I'm back!

Contents

9. Connecting on the Phone

10. Connecting in Writing

11. Using the 'Net' to Connect

Acknowledgements

My thanks go first to Gill Bailey and Krystyna Mayer of Piatkus for both their patience and persistence in helping me to develop the concept for this book, and to my agent, Liz Puttick, for doing her job so professionally and well.

I am particularly grateful to my great pal Kim Carey for her skills in typing the manuscript and to Carmel Maloney and Paula Ledbury for producing the finishing touches. The graphics wouldn't have been the same had it not been for my good friend Will Yearsley's excellent support. My heartfelt thanks to you all.

Equally important has been the input of all of those professionals who have attended my networking and working the room courses over the last seven years. Your input has been instrumental in moulding my thinking and ensuring that what I say in these pages actually works in real life. In effect I have simply captured the essence of our discussions and created a blueprint of actions that I know will stand the test in the world of big – and small – business.

I am also indebted to the 'gurus' of various aspects of networking who are featured in these pages, including Meribeth Bunch on aspects of confidence and presence, Guy Levine on using email to connect effectively and world memory champ

David Thomas on remembering names and faces. Finally, thanks to great mentors Tony Tighe and David Maister – you are true exponents of the craft.

Introduction

WE'VE ALL HEARD 'It's not what you know, it's who you know' and today this age-old saying has never had more truth.

A few years back networking was seen as something that people did in a haphazard and unstructured way – you were just lucky if you happened to 'hit it off' with people who were later in a position to help you. Now things have changed. *Network Your Way to Success* will show you that there is both an art and a real science to developing wonderful social and business relationships.

What Networking Is – and Isn't

You'll no doubt be pretty familiar with the term 'networking' and with the people who do it. You'll see networkers in all guises and in all walks of life. As experienced networkers know, nothing can move your business or career faster and more effectively than having a base of contacts who are in the right position to help you to achieve your ambitions. On the other hand, there are few things more personally rewarding than to use your skills, knowledge and contacts to help *others* to achieve their goals too.

When you connect with others in this way it's one of the most emotionally and financially rewarding methods of doing business.

Networking with others in person, on the telephone and in writing keeps you plugged into your key contacts – those people who can help you to get the inside track on business opportunities, give you sound advice, help you to find a new role or identify an alternative supplier. They are the same people who will act as cheerleaders when you're up and as a springboard when you're down. And, here's the big point, you can do the same for them too, because you are part of *their* network.

Networking is a process that can be used by anyone in any aspect of life. You can apply the same techniques that have earned people millions in business to develop your personal relationships and help you to achieve whatever you want to do. Whether you are a contract worker or a consultant, a business owner or an employee, a part-time worker or a housewife, adopting the networking mindset works every time. As you'll discover in these pages, it's almost certain that you are undervaluing the opportunities available to you and not fully utilising the personal skills and relationship 'assets' you already possess.

If you feel intrigued and excited by the possibilities, you have every right to be, because when you take the relationship-building techniques of the champion business networkers and apply them to your own situation, you almost can't help being more successful.

I make no apologies for putting relationship building in the context of business, because I believe that each of us is really a business, whether we own a company or not.

Think of it like this: whatever your role in life, you have to 'sell' yourself to someone else.

- **As an individual** If you want relationships you have to 'sell' yourself to the other person and show them the benefits of being with you.

- **As an employee** You have to sell yourself to your employer to be recognised, gain promotion or even keep your job.

- **As a business** You have to convince a customer or client to buy the benefits you are offering rather than those of your competitors.

I'm not talking here about hard-nosed selling or making contacts for mercenary and self-serving reasons. Instead my goal in these pages is to show you what people with integrity do to maximise the benefit of their interactions with people. I want to give you an insight into the pleasure, achievement and, yes, financial gain that can be yours once you know how to connect effectively.

As a marketing director with the world's largest business advisory firm, PricewaterhouseCoopers, I've been leading networking courses for clients and our own professionals for nearly ten years. I've trained thousands of people, but equally importantly, I've had the opportunity to talk with them about the business and social challenges they face and the techniques they use to get results. So this is a practical book based on practical experience of what works in developing business relationships. The techniques work in real life, not just in theory.

Introducing the 'Connector'

This book takes a peek into the attributes of the top networkers, the ones who've taken the process to much greater heights. I call them 'connectors', because they fulfil the deeper dictionary definition of what networking with a focus is all about. My job here is to help you to become one of them by highlighting what skills they have and how they use them to get results – whether it's winning 'big ticket' work or developing a wonderful relationship.

IN PRACTICE

The first chief executive I ever had when I started working in the public relations business was one Tony Tighe, who ran a UK-based consultancy called GTPR. Tony built his entire business – the sale of which made him a multi-millionare a few years back – on the strength of his relationships with his contacts. He never advertised once and hardly ever did any form of traditional marketing with brochures, sales letters and the like.

What he did do, to the point of brilliance, was to maintain fantastic relationships with his clients, his suppliers and other professionals. That's not all. Work came flooding in from Tony's old school and university chums, the guys at the golf club, the person he met on the plane to Heathrow, the next-door neighbour who had attended the barbecue at his house two weeks earlier, a friend of a friend, a client of a client, and so on... It also came in from the people he met when he did his PR presentations (Tony was a great presenter) and quite simply from the profile he had by being out in the market.

Tony was charismatic. He enjoyed people. He was a connector. Tony Tighe built his business on networking alone – and you can do the same.

Since those early days with Tony, and having worked at the highest level in professional services firms, consultancies and multi-national businesses, I have seen at first hand the difference that effective connecting can make to the success of organisations and the individuals within them.

There are very few good networkers – and that's great news for you, because by learning the techniques used by those who stand head and shoulders above the crowd you can achieve excellent results very quickly.

There is no mystery about it – anyone can be an effective connector if they know how. They can become comfortable with the tried, tested and proven networking skills used by the experts – the 'rainmakers' who regularly bring in new pieces of work for their organisation and almost invariably know the right movers and shakers.

So What Does 'Connecting' Mean?

Let's be clear from the outset about what connecting is all about. Check out this extract from the *Collins English Dictionary*:

Connect
1. to link or be linked together, join, fasten
2. to relate or associate
3. to establish communications with or between

From Latin connectere, *to bind together*

Connection
1. the act or state of connecting, union
2. something that connects, joins or relates; link or bond
3. a relationship or association
4. logical sequence of thought or expression, coherence
5. an acquaintance, esp. one who has influence and prestige
6. communications link between two points

What Skills Does the Connector Have?

Communication

- Can persuade, in writing, on the phone and in meetings and presentations.

- Keeps in regular touch with contacts.

- Is a great questioner and listener.

Personal skills

- Knows how to create great rapport.

- Uses body language effectively.

- Knows what to say and when to say it.

Attitude

- Can 'stand in another's shoes'.

- Has a positive approach to life.

- Plays a part in their network.

- Is willing to offer help.

- Makes the most of their network, for themselves and others.

Making Your Contacts Your Most Valuable Asset

In networking, you get back what you give. And you can't give a lot unless you make the effort to understand your contacts' hopes and dreams, needs and wants, and become tuned into their views, principles, goals and objectives. Once you understand these and provide the answers more obviously than anyone else, then business and social success are yours.

Focusing on how you can help others in order to help yourself is a fundamental shift in perception that marks the real connectors out from the rest.

IN PRACTICE

Andersen, the business advisory firm, together with research consultancy DYG Inc., conducted a survey of senior corporate executives to determine which types of relationship they considered to be most essential to business success.

Customer and employee relationships were clearly the most important sources of value, according to the findings. But, more surprisingly, the research highlighted a widespread disconnection between those beliefs and the actions of senior executives.

'Executives certainly realise the importance of their customer and other market relationships, yet they are not taking a proactive approach to managing these incredible sources of value,' said

Barrie Libert, the director of the research project. 'Today's increasingly networked economy requires that all companies build intimate relationships with their customers, employees, suppliers and others in the market who can influence their fortunes – as well as use emerging technologies to connect these relationships throughout the enterprise in order to realise unprecedented value.'

Ninety-five per cent of the executives surveyed said that 'acquiring and maintaining relationships with customers' was essential to business success, *but* only 54 per cent of those executives' companies had strategies in place to build one-to-one relationships with customers. Hmm...

What This Book Can Do for You

Network Your Way to Success is a relationship-building blueprint for anyone in business who is under pressure to deliver new clients and generate income, make the most of their existing contacts and develop new ones. Specifically, it can help:

- Newcomers to serious networking who want to understand what it's all about and how to do it.

- People in organisations who want to be recognised for their contribution.

- Directors, executives, managers and salespeople who are expected to represent their organisations in the marketplace and at business functions.

- Consultants, portfolio workers, interim managers, freelancers and others who rely on referrals.

- All who are involved in 'hosting' the events their business holds.

Networking is simply about building rapport and alliances, creating a group of contacts with whom you can build a business and personal relationship. It's the most cost-effective and personally rewarding marketing tool around – when it is used wisely and professionally. But it's a skill that takes knowledge and practice to perfect. Luckily, these pages are packed with practical tips that can turn a novice into a master. You will learn:

People skills

How to:

- 'Work a room', make new contacts and gain their permission to stay in touch.

- Be a great host, greet people with impact and develop rapport with them.

- Elegantly turn a social chat into a business discussion.

- Create a lasting impression.

Networking techniques

How to:

- Quickly build on your existing network and make the most of every contact opportunity.

- Avoid cultural and etiquette 'gaffes'.

- Effectively use your contacts database to generate a stream of referrals.

- Follow up with finesse – and great success.

- Make your contacts your most valuable personal and business asset.

Communication skills

How to:

- Communicate effectively in meetings, on the phone, in writing and in presentations.

- Develop your client-handling skills.

- Improve your persuasiveness.

- Use keeping in touch as a way of generating assignments and opportunities.

IN PRACTICE

When you're connecting effectively with your network of contacts it's far easier to call people you've not yet met. It opens doors, warms up prospects and 'thaws' cold calls.

Which of these two telephone calls would you prefer – and which is likely to get the better response?

'Hello, I'm John Timperley. I'm calling to tell you about the design services we offer.'

or

'Hello, I'm John Timperley. I was speaking with a mutual acquaintance, Bob Jones, yesterday, and he recommended that I give you a call. I understand from Bob that you may be looking for a designer to help you on a project.'

Knowing Bob definitely warms up the conversation and provides a platform for, at the very least, a cordial discussion ... one that could lead to a new business opportunity.

Making the Most of the Book

While many of the connector's moves are subtle, I've attempted to capture them and put them under the microscope in a logical order, from looking at your existing contacts and connecting style to creating the right impression, and then homing in on the various ways in which the connector excels when communicating with people socially, in their organisations, in meetings, on the phone, in writing, over the Internet and in creating new opportunities.

You can go through the steps in this order. But if you prefer, the book is designed to allow you to skim the contents page and pick a section that grabs your attention. Each section is a stand-alone lesson in its own right. And in each section there are 'In Practice' examples of how the techniques have been applied in real life by real people and organisations. You've seen a couple already.

Each section also has 'Try This' exercises designed to actively involve you in developing your network and your skills, and there is a 'Connector's Toolkit' section at appropriate junctures to give you a review or a sheaf of quickfire tips you can use straight away.

Naturally you'll want to incorporate those ideas you feel comfortable with into your business and social encounters, but don't forget some of the others either. Just because you are uncomfortable with a particular approach just now doesn't mean that you will feel the same about it once you have more experience and confidence under your belt. These techniques have worked for others and can work for you too.

IN PRACTICE

An office equipment supplier recently undertook a review of their business and identified all of their lapsed customers from the last five years. These were people who had bought products from them previously but for whatever reason has stopped purchasing. The business had simply lost contact with its customers in the same way that you may lose contact with a friend – there's no particular reason, but you've just drifted apart and not had the time or the opportunity to reconnect.

Knowing that it is far easier to sell to an existing contact than to create a new customer, the company's canny marketing director launched a campaign to recontact all of those lapsed customers. The marketing department sent letters and followed up by phone to find out the reasons why people hadn't been buying from them lately. Some people had moved jobs within their business, others had changed organisations, some had found alternative suppliers and others just didn't have the product at the front of their mind.

These reasons aren't important. The point is that in reconnecting with their former customers the supplier got a huge amount of new information that was helpful in understanding what their customers wanted. But here's the result: the £100,000 exercise generated more than £2m in extra sales immediately, because the organisation had simply taken the time to find out how its contacts were doing and how it could help them now.

Think about the sales in the years ahead now that those contacts have been reunited with their supplier. You can do the same with the whole range of other important contacts in your life.

As we'll see, a network is something that we have all established around us. Connectors use and develop their network in order to extract the greatest value – not just financial, but emotional and social too. With the offer of help and a friendly disposition, they also feature strongly in other people's networks – but they are only successful because they see things first and foremost from the mindset of giving, not getting.

Let's have a look now at your existing contacts and how you can become 'better connected'.

CHAPTER 1

Getting Connected

IRST THE GREAT NEWS – you are already well connected! One of the problems many would-be connectors experience when they begin networking is acquiring new contacts outside their own field of existing contacts. But you already have better connections than you think.

Your existing networking 'assets' are all the relationships you have built, in particular those which are current and active. All of these are connected to all kinds of relationships with all sorts of additional people – people who may be your next client or be in a position to send opportunities your way.

We all have a vast network of contacts already, but some of these are forgotten, neglected or ignored. Research shows that almost everyone knows between 250 and 500 people on a first-name basis. You may know many more. If you have a bit of healthy scepticism at this point, try listing all your contacts (you'll find a detailed template to help you on the opposite page). Include in the list your current business colleagues, past colleagues, clients, suppliers and acquaintances. Move on to friends, wider family members, members of any associations and clubs you belong to and past schoolfriends. If you have children, include their friends' parents and you'll easily have 250 people.

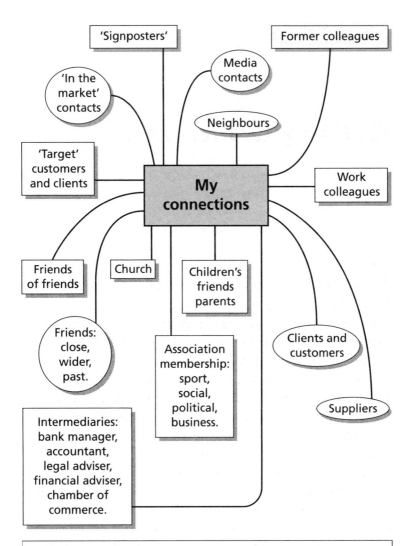

'Signposters'

Former colleagues

Media contacts

'In the market' contacts

Neighbours

'Target' customers and clients

My connections

Work colleagues

Friends of friends

Church

Children's friends parents

Clients and customers

Friends: close, wider, past.

Association membership: sport, social, political, business.

Suppliers

Intermediaries: bank manager, accountant, legal adviser, financial adviser, chamber of commerce.

Try this

Produce your own network diagram and write down the names of your key contacts under the various headings.

Then ask yourself:
- Who else should I know and how can I meet them?
- What does this pattern tell me about my existing contacts?
- How many of these people would it be helpful and enjoyable to re-establish contact with?

So, if we say that on average each person knows 300 people and each of those knows another 300 people, you technically have easy access to 90,000 people. Now that's powerful!

Assessing Your Own Connecting Style

Thank goodness we're not all the same. We don't act or think in the same way and we don't all share the same goals and vision. Nevertheless, unless your objective is to be a hermit and live on top of a mountain, connecting is for everyone.

Before we swing into how to connect, let's take a peek at *why* you would want to do it, *what* aspects will appeal to you most and *how* to get the greatest benefit from the time you spend connecting with others.

If you had to boil connecting down into the reasons why you want to do it, you'd get four 'camps'. You may find that you'll have a foot in more than one camp, but let's see... People connect with others for:

- Business.

- Relationships.

- Ideas.

- Learning.

Let's prise these categories open a little and see what kind of people tend to be in there...

Business: 'show me the money ...'

In this category are those people who use connecting to win more work, build their business and develop their career. They are usually great at spotting new opportunities and working with their contacts to get results.

Normally, though not always, business connectors are very focused and can, if they aren't careful, appear to be using others to achieve their goals. They tend to place less emphasis on nurturing long-term relationships unless their contacts are consistently helpful.

Relationships: 'getting to know you...'

Maybe you're more of a relationship connector who finds it easy to develop rapport with people and understand their needs. If this sounds like you, you'll probably also be a great coach and supporter of your contacts and good at keeping in regular contact with them. The relationship itself, wherever it takes you, will be the most important thing.

On the other side of the coin you might find yourself thinking that you are a bit slow in asking for the business when opportunities present themselves and, indeed, are not the fastest out of the starting-blocks when it comes to initiating serious business contacts.

Learning: 'teach me, teacher...'

Are you connecting for your own personal development purposes, to learn a new skill perhaps, or simply to be around others in your sphere who may be in a position to act as a mentor or coach? Normally such a connector is wonderful with others of similar mindset and a super source of information on their area of interest.

The reverse also applies – if you fit this category you may have little time for those who can't add anything to your knowledge or aren't interested in your area. There's also the possibility that you'll be so focused on learning that you don't apply what you know to real situations, or you have only a hazy view of how your knowledge might benefit your own career.

Ideas: 'what do you think of this?'

If you're an ideas connector you'll love networking with others in your field to get fresh thinking, to debate issues and basically swap thoughts on an intellectual or technical level. You'll be concentrating on the power of ideas and concepts and devote less time to building relationships for the sake of them. Because of your thirst for the new, you'll keep close to those who keep coming up with the breakthroughs, but tend to drift away from those whose ideas are 'old hat'.

If you recognise yourself here, you may also see that you would benefit from a greater drive to do something tangible with the ideas you have discussed. You may have the feeling that you really must keep in contact with others who don't have the ideas of the moment but deserve a closer connecting relationship as a person, not just a source of ideas and information. While this is, of course, stereotyping people quite outrageously in the daily newspaper 'horoscope' style, like all good analyses (astrological or otherwise), it has hopefully got you thinking about why you connect and the positives and possible pitfalls of each approach.

From past experience I know that your response will range from 'That's me to a tee in the business category' through to 'I connect for business, relationship, learning *and* ideas reasons and don't consider myself to be in any box.' Good for you! Any permutation is fine.

The key question to stop and ask yourself occasionally is: 'Which box does my connecting activity fit into – and what do I need to do to get the greatest benefit, bearing in mind the potential pitfalls in each?'

How You Connect

While there are four main reasons *why* we network, the key determinant of *how* you connect is your personality.

You've no doubt heard about the psychological segmentation of people into 'extroverts' or 'introverts'. The brilliant news is that both sets of people can participate fully in connecting. You may be surprised to know that extroverts are not necessarily better networkers, they simply do it differently. So, before we leave this section, let's gain a bit of insight into the behaviour of extroverts and introverts as it relates to connecting with others. And the big question is: which are you?

TRY THIS

An extrovert connector

- Likes making new contacts.

- Is confident socially.

- Likes talking better than writing (and listening).

- Has many contacts.

- Leads the relationship building.

- Likes to be in the spotlight.

- Is interested in people first, ideas second.

- Brainstorms easily with others.

An introvert connector

- Is more comfortable with existing contacts.

- Is slower to take the initiative socially.

- Prefers writing (and listening) to talking.

- Has a few, very good, contacts.

- Prefers to see how a relationship develops.

- Would rather be in the audience than on centre stage.

- Finds that ideas are paramount, with people a close second.

- Is more comfortable generating ideas alone.

As you would expect, many people display characteristics of both extroverts and introverts and often how they react differs with each situation. For some reason most people appear to be more extrovert after a couple of glasses of wine!

The principle is sound that extroverts have something to learn from introverts in the areas of building deeper relationships, listening better and connecting on the ideas level. Conversely, the introverts among us will recognise that there are times when being more outgoing and sharing ideas would be really advantageous.

Throughout this book we'll be learning techniques that have been used by great connectors, both extrovert and introvert, to help themselves and their contacts to achieve their goals. You can adapt them as much as you like to suit your own particular style.

TRY THIS

Think about how you presently meet people and review the effectiveness of these approaches. Then consider what alternatives are possible and how much better they may be in helping you to achieve your connecting goals.

Connecting at Work

To have a high profile within and outside your organisation you have to communicate effectively with others. Even if you work alone, you'll still have a network of people who are important to you as suppliers of work, new business leads, information and support. At the other end of the scale, perhaps you work in a multi-national organisation and your challenge is just to understand how best you can interact with others at your level in different aspects of the business.

Either way, almost every person in employment has to ask themselves: 'How do I get noticed for the contribution I make?' and, equally: 'What can I do to help others who would value my skills and knowledge?' For more experienced connectors, the challenge revolves around: 'How can I promote myself and my specialist skills in a way that is not self-serving but demonstrates that I am a contributor to my sector, specialism, business or department?'

Let's plunge straight in with some advice for those in larger organisations, then cover what everyone can do to be better known in the outside market. We'll also touch on the best way to let people know that you are on the lookout for a fresh challenge and the value of using the best personal advertisement you'll ever have – a business card.

'Get the big flag out – I exist in here!'

It's easy to be anonymous in a large organisation and with increasing industry consolidation and globalisation you can easily become a small (and unknown) cog in a very large machine. The antidote centres around getting involved and genuinely 'adding' value.

To become visible, try these for starters:

■ **Volunteer for projects** you believe in and feel you can contribute to. They will often be led by senior figures in your organisation and include a range of people from other disciplines in the business. It's your chance to work with others in a way you may not have done previously and to demonstrate your capabilities and commitment. Often such volunteer projects, because of their lack of hierarchy, present a great opportunity for you to learn, grow, participate and develop new skills.

IN PRACTICE

Lesley was a marketing assistant with an international company when she volunteered for a role as a publicist for a charity project the company was involved with alongside other 'blue chip' businesses in the area. From being a relatively junior marketing professional with potential, within six months she had met (and was on first-name terms with) all of the chief executives and marketing directors of those organisations. She had built working relationships with all of the heads of the regional TV, radio, newspapers and magazines, and in fact had better contacts than any of her bosses as a result!

Naturally, she gained immensely in confidence and credibility during this time, but most important of all she had demonstrated her ability to some of the key decision-makers in the area. Little wonder that she was soon promoted within her own firm and was eventually 'headhunted' for a much bigger marketing role.

- **Get involved** in your organisation's sports, charity and social activities. They are a great chance to mix with colleagues from different departments. You'll get to know others and be known.

- **Use your lunchtimes to mix** If you have a company restaurant, eat in there; if not, eat out. Either way, don't sit with your same old people all the time. Meet other colleagues for lunch just as you would if you were meeting an external supplier or customer. Get to know them and their area of business better – and share their interests, hobbies and family matters. It doesn't have to be all work!

- **Be a 'buddy'** Many organisations formalise networking among peers in different departments or divisions through a 'buddy' system whereby they are encouraged to keep in regular touch with one or more colleagues as part of their work objectives. It's a great way to keep everyone involved in internal networking at a level they are comfortable with.

- **Get creative** If you have a suggestion scheme, suggest something and keep the ideas flowing. You may be financially rewarded for your best ones, but even if not, your regular contribution of 'fresh thinking' won't go unnoticed. You'll be seen, rightly, as someone who is very interested and keen.

- **Be publicly noticed** If you have a newsletter, contribute something – even if it's only a story idea. But why not be brave and have a go at writing yourself? And send a photo too! You could become the correspondent or spokesperson for your area of the business, someone the editor relies on for good stories. Being a correspondent in this way opens doors for you. You can talk to almost anyone in your organisation (even outside it too) when you are on a mission to research and write stories for your company magazine. It's a fantastic way to get to know people and their views.

TRY THIS

Give some thought to your existing profile in your organisation or department.

- Is your profile high enough?

- What else could you do to raise it? (The ideas above are a start.)

- Do you know your counterparts in other parts of the business, or at your competitors?

- Which outside bodies are you involved with and are they meeting your networking objectives?

- Are you in a position to get a higher profile for your work, or for your other activities?

Get into the Market

The 'get involved' advice applies to getting involved in the outside world too – but be selective. There are many really beneficial organisations to choose from – and there are an equal number that will suck away your time, leaving you little to show for your efforts. Consider the merits of the following and any others relevant to your situation, and prioritise those that you think will give you most benefit and enjoyment: chambers of trade and commerce, business networking associations, the Round Table, the Rotary Club, charity fundraising organisations and industry associations. These are just some of the options – you will be able to find many more. If you need help, ask your local librarian. Try the following avenues too:

- **Go to trade shows** If you are in an appropriate sector, a visit to the key trade shows can help you to build a wealth of contacts in your industry or profession very quickly indeed. The secret is to follow up any contacts made, so that you start to build a bond and your name stands out from the dozens – possibly hundreds – of people your new-found contacts met at the show. When you are there, if it's mutually beneficial, offer to meet your fledgling friends for lunch or coffee to help cement the relationship more quickly.

- **Attend relevant 'thought leadership' conferences and workshops** To avoid wasting your time, be selective in what you attend. Big hitters and key influencers in your industry will only attend the strategic 'big picture' stuff, not the tactical skills update programmes. If you want to be seen as a big thinker and a strategist, find out what the gurus of the industry are saying ... and be prepared to form your own view.

- **Publicise yourself** The champion connectors create a name for themselves by developing a public profile. Ultimately, if you want to be recognised for what you do you will probably need to get involved with the media. Those who have appeared in the press or on radio and TV know the power of such publicity. They'll have taken calls from people who have seen or heard them – friends, contacts, old pals and possibly new business acquaintances too.

- **Comment regularly on matters in which you want to be seen as an expert** This will soon cement your position as someone who knows their stuff. If you become an established authority, people relevant to the subject area will actively seek you out to network with – a Nirvana situation for a connector.

IN PRACTICE

Organisations can network too. The grocery industry in Europe is a highly concentrated industry with small profit margins. Feeling the squeeze between supermarket chains and dominant national suppliers, EUROSELECT, a network of 12 grocery wholesalers, was set up. By exchanging 'buy' suggestions and product prices, the wholesalers can:

- Strengthen their competitive position – they no longer have to compete alone.

- Reduce their dependency on suppliers – they can source from other countries.

Now if a Greek member learns from the network that cans of Pepsi are cheaper in Spain, they can place their order via EUROSELECT to obtain the better price.

Making the most of formal and informal networks

As we've seen already, there is a multitude of organisations and events that promote networking. But it's vital that you take some time to evaluate how useful they will be to you and, equally important, review how much you enjoyed them. If you decide to join a formal society or club, make sure that you get involved. It's usually better to focus on one group properly than to spread yourself too thinly and achieve little in the way of meaningful contacts. The key question to ask yourself at this stage is: where can I meet people who can introduce me to the contacts I want to meet?

Whether you are self-employed or an employee, a one-man band or part of a multi-national set-up, getting out and meeting people who can help your business is a key skill for the budding business dynamo. And without doubt, successful people see networking as a key business-building skill. This has been borne out by scientific research in Australia with entrepreneurial companies. The findings showed a very strong relationship between networking and profit growth. In fact, networking produced the strongest predictor of long-term business success.

Sounds promising, but you also have to be very careful about the way you do it. You can spend as much time networking poorly and attending inappropriate events and meetings as you can in working closely with others who can help you to develop your business and social contacts. For example, going to the local chamber of commerce meeting to hear someone give a lecture might qualify as networking, but unless your customers or clients are local, it's likely to be an unproductive use of your business contact-making time – although, on the social side, you might meet the love of your life there!

Constantly ask yourself what you are likely to get out of your networking time. Here are some ideas to help you to focus your efforts.

Ask a 'signposter' which way to go

In every organisation, sector or city there are people who know what is happening. These 'signposters' are at the interface where many networks meet and overlap – they might belong to industry bodies, employers' associations, local business support organisations or just be people who get about and know others who may be helpful to you.

Once you have found these key people, absorb them into your network. They can help you overcome difficulties and open up new opportunities simply because of the store of formal and informal knowledge they hold. When you ask signposters for help, you are making connections with their own networks – which could indeed be extensive. Signposters can be the most valuable contacts you have.

The information signposters provide is just as likely to be informal as formal. For example, bank managers can give you formal information on how to organise your accounts to maximise the interest on your bank. But they'll also know many local business people and be aware of opportunities you may not have heard of. If your business is offering a service or a product, they might know someone who is looking for just that. Think about who the signposters may be in your organisation, sector, profession or town, and make contact with them.

David Hall, an entrepreneurial guru and author of *In the Company of Heroes: An Insider's Guide to Entrepreneurs at Work*, has this advice for connectors who want to use networking to develop their business (much of this can be adapted by connectors who want to network within their own organisation):

Make a list of your existing contacts

These might include:

- Key customers.

- Suppliers.

- Your bank manager.

- Business contacts.

- Advisers (official and unofficial).

Once you have done this, consider whether your list is as comprehensive as it should be. Then list the people *you* may be able to help, so that you maintain a balanced approach to your networking.

Widen your network

The success step now is to extend your network to include people who can help you resolve business problems, spot opportunities or act as signposters to new contacts, customers or clients. How do you go about it? Talking to entrepreneurs about how they made these contacts often throws up a range of possibilities, according to David Hall. These include local entrepreneurs' forums, whether informal or formal set-ups, small business clubs and enterprise agency forums.

The key to making the most of these meetings is not going along with the attitude of just taking advice from others. The most successful connectors make it a two-way exchange, providing information, advice and input to others as well as gaining some insight into approaches they may wish to take in their own business.

Add customers and clients to your contacts list too. Ask where they gather their information about suppliers like you. Find out who, or what, influences their thinking and whom they turn to for advice. Some contacts will be far more useful to you than others because they too will belong to networks. Where appropriate, add these key players to your network as well.

Last, but not least, you will also have access to some special business advisers like your bank manager, your lawyer and your accountant, whose livelihood ultimately depends on business people like yourself. Ask their advice on who you should be talking to and which formal associations you could become involved with. It's a good litmus test to see if they themselves have tapped into successful networks.

Cultivate it

Put your edited list of contacts in your address book or, better still, onto your computer database and aim to keep in touch with each contact at least once a quarter. Find out what interests them and when you find relevant information, call them or send it in the post or via the Net with a personal note. Remember that connecting is a two-way street and you need to nurture your contacts. You can't call in favours from contacts if you haven't spoken to them for 18 months!

Play your part and say thanks

Now that you have established a relationship with your key contacts you can ask for help when you need it, but be sure to thank them if they do help you. Thanking people needn't cost much, but will repay itself many times over in future favours. On the other side of the coin, be sure to make time to help others. Successful networking is a 'win–win' situation, so if one of your connections wants help and advice, be prepared to go out of your way to support them.

Connecting to Get a Job – or a New Opportunity

Being well connected to your network gives you a ten-yard start over your counterparts when opportunities appear. It gives you an inside track (not an unfair advantage) in moving laterally or being promoted within your organisation or finding a new role somewhere else. It also helps you to be in a good position if your company reorganises and the effects don't look as though they are going to be in your favour. Losing your job doesn't have the stigma it once had, but nevertheless having a strong network can often cushion the blow and make the 'bounce back' so much easier. Indeed, most people today will have several jobs and two or three major career changes in their working lives. A connector's network can be both a safety net and a trampoline at such times.

That said, the prerequisite is that you are good at what you do. No one wants to recommend or support a 'weak link'.

So, assuming you know your stuff, what can your work in developing connections do for you?

TRY THIS

Many jobs (some surveys say over 75 per cent) are never actually advertised and, of course, your possibilities of success rise significantly if you've been given a personal reference by an influential contact.

The connecting you do externally will help you to raise your profile. A good litmus test to see if you are doing enough connecting in the right areas is to ask yourself these three 'killer' questions:

1. Do my organisation's competitors know about me and my role?
2. What do they think of me?
3. If a more senior job with a competitor arose, would I be in prime position to be offered the role (or even headhunted)?

It's even been known for a job to be created especially for a person whose skills are known and valued. At the very least a referral from a contact will get you away from a 'cold' start and push the door half open for you. The rest, of course, is up to you.

Ask for support from your 'fans'

Your business and personal contacts can become your greatest supporters and champions when you are changing jobs or looking for a new opportunity. But remember, you can only ask for help from people you have built relationships with. Suddenly asking someone for a favour after two years of non-communication is not the best platform on which to re-establish rapport.

This highlights the importance of maintaining regular contact with your wider networks. If you are in the unfortunate position of having to ask for a favour from someone you have lost touch with, the elegant approach is to reconnect first and then, if appropriate, ask for help later in the relationship.

When seeking new opportunities, make it known, subtly, that you may be open to a new challenge inside or outside your organisation. Make sure you are clear which you want. If you are looking for a role with a new company, don't go scattering your CV all over town – that's not the mark of a professional business person and smacks of desperation. The smarter connector's move is to make enquires with relevant network contacts regarding their knowledge of opportunities which fit your goals for your future. Pass on your CV only if you both feel there is something concrete to do with it. This is a delicate process, so have some decorum.

Hear it on the grapevine

Often the key to getting a new position is knowing what's going on. That requires you to have a strong and wide network of contacts, including a couple of headhunter friends if possible (I kid you not!) and to be tapped into the communication between appropriate folk in your town, sector or specialism.

A full address book that's never used is a cardinal sin for a connector, so make sure you keep in touch with your contacts and add value to them when you can.

Get out there

Last, but not least, be proactive. Don't sit and wait for news to come to you. Keep up to speed with all the key local, national and industry developments. Read the papers, identify opportunities for yourself and others in your network to win new business or create potential new openings. That's what connecting is all about. It's not a blinkered 'What's in it for me?' approach. A wider 'How can I help myself and others?' horizon is what sorts the great connectors from the pack. On that basis you'll thoroughly deserve your new role.

IN PRACTICE

Big businesses usually have sophisticated contact programmes for their 'alumni' – people who used to be employed by them who have now gone to work elsewhere. Good as these corporate programmes can be, the irony is that on occasions the businesses, when presenting for new work to these alumni contacts, find that they have not maintained effective relationships with them and instead of being 'warm' to their former employer, they are now extremely cold. They believe (possibly rightly) that contact has been renewed with them only because there's a sniff of new business in the air.

Nobody likes to feel used, so the moral is to keep your contacts going; it's great fun and, ultimately, great business sense.

Using Your Business Cards for Maximum Effect

If you are networking effectively, your business card can be your most potent long-term relationship builder and your smallest, cheapest and most effective advertisement.

'Hang on,' you might be saying, 'I don't have a card, and I'm not sure that I need one.' I understand that point of view, but read on to see if I can convince you. Once you get into networking, even within your own organisation, you'll need a mechanism to remind people who you are and what you do – and often the best answer is to have a card which provides this information. What's more, it's never been easier to obtain one. Wander into any high street fast-print or copy shop and they'll do them quickly for you. I've even seen machines at service stations and rail terminals that allow you to print your own cards on the spot. So, even if your own business only allows the 'top brass' to have a card, think about capturing your details on one you create yourself. It will help your social and business networking enormously.

Your card is a reflection of you as an individual and an extension of your organisation's image. Whip yours out now (or someone else's if you don't have one). What does it say to you about you and your business? Is it projecting the image and message you want? While you're at it, have someone independent scrutinise it too. What do they see as an objective observer?

While going through this apparently banal exercise in my networking seminars some delegates, on taking a fresh look at their card, decide that a revamp is in order. They've maybe compared theirs with others which, in addition to carrying the basic information of name, business, location and contact numbers, have also been more creative in including product or service details on the reverse. Some cards even feature a company philosophy and mission, a photograph on the front, special offers and even an unusual promotion whereby if the recipient of the card calls a special customer hotline number, they receive complimentary samples of a well-known cosmetic product!

The point is, within the confines of your sector and the image you wish to convey, there is likely to be more you can do to present yourself so that the recipient has a mini brochure of what you do, why you do it and the real benefits of knowing you.

No one ever said your card has to be normal size – I've seen all sorts of shapes and dimensions in my time, even outsize ones that are folded in half to fit in the standard cardholders.

Your card may or may not need a revamp, but whatever you do, use it effectively.

Stock up and stash away

Top connectors *always* have enough business cards with them. Not for them the embarrassment of having to write their name on a scrap of paper or a napkin, or the indignity of having to borrow a card from their conversation partner and sheepishly writing their own basic details on the reverse. Most connectors have probably suffered this indignity at some time or other and vowed 'Never again.' That's why they have a supply of cards in their suit, their briefcase, the glove compartment of their car, their computer case and even a side pocket of their sports bag. Most likely they'll really look the part, as I recommend you do, by having their cards in a special cardholder. These are not expensive (unless you insist on gold!) but really do convey that you take your networking seriously.

Serious golfers wouldn't dream of wandering the fairways with no head covers to protect their wooden clubs. Likewise, the ace connector doesn't turn up to a meeting with loose and dog-eared business cards.

Keep them handy

Male connectors have a slight advantage over their female counterparts when it comes to cards, simply because they have more options on where to keep them. For women, suit jacket pockets are often sewn up or non-existent, and handbags are the next best bet.

Clearly, despite what I said just a moment ago, having cards in your briefcase, car or desk drawer is as helpful as a chocolate fireguard when you are at a function or in a meeting and are asked for a card. You need cards secreted about your person. For males this is usually in a jacket pocket. The top pocket appears to be favourite with many. Others go for the inside jacket pocket or the old favourite, the wallet. The sophisticated connector will, of course, simply draw their silver card-case from its usual location and elegantly hand over their card.

Give yours by asking for theirs

If you want to give a card to someone, ask for theirs! It's not as crazy as it sounds. Asking your conversation partner, or the person you've just introduced yourself to, for a card is polite – it shows that your interest in them is your first priority.

If they have a card with them, they'll almost certainly give it to you, and usually ask for yours in return. If they don't request one, it's an easy step for you to proffer yours by saying, 'And here's mine.'

If they haven't a card with them, simply say: 'Can I offer you mine?' They'll be embarrassed that they haven't got theirs to hand, but grateful that you've provided your details to them. If you really do want their details, why not give them an extra card of yours and ask them to jot down the essentials on the reverse? But make sure that you put it somewhere safe and draw a line though your details on the front to avoid mistakenly giving it away later.

A great, and appropriate, chance to ask for a card is when you are nearing the end of a conversation. 'It's been really interesting talking to you... Have you got a card?'

Flip it and capture key information

Nowadays it is socially acceptable to write on the back of someone's card – unless you are dealing with contacts from Far Eastern cultures like China and Japan, where all business cards should be treated with extreme reverence, and 'defacing' them by writing on them is the height of insult (as is putting them in your trouser pocket). So reserve this writing technique for contacts in Western cultures – and even then it is polite to ask permission in advance: 'Would you mind if I made a note of what we've just agreed on the back of your card so that I can capture the key points?'

Top connectors take this approach to capturing details. Then, as soon as possible after meeting a promising new contact (usually in the office or later at home, but occasionally at the event if the situation permits), they'll take out the card and will jot down information that has the potential to transform their relationship with their conversation partner.

What do they do? They'll flip the card over and write the date of the meeting and the event/occasion. They'll make a note of who made the introduction or who led the event, then they'll capture the highlights of the discussion and any relevant information. Naturally, they'll put down any actions they have agreed and, if they are really smart, they'll insert a 'memory jogger' to help them remember the name of their new contact so that they won't get caught out next time they meet.

It sounds a lot, but you'll be amazed what information you can squeeze on a card and how the best connectors use it to cement a relationship.

IN PRACTICE

Let's walk through an example. Assume I've just met Jackie, business development director for a computer systems supplier. We had a very short but pleasant conversation at a charity lunch held by the MD of a local company, Flowsafe. I've handed Jackie my card and suggested that it would be worthwhile if she sent some literature on her business to me. Here's what she wrote on the back of my card later that day:

12/10/01 Flowsafe Charity event (£8k raised)

- Introduction by Jack Walsh, MD.

- Send information on services.

- John has supplier already.

- Busy with new product marketing.

- Going on holiday to France.

- Three girls.

- Dark hair, moustache.

Here's Jackie's covering letter to me enclosing her literature. Note that it's not over-familiar, but demonstrates that she has been listening to me sufficiently to be able to demonstrate that she is different. Contrast it with the usual 'standard' letter enclosing literature.

Dear John

It was a pleasure to talk to you at the Flowsafe charity event. Knowing Jack Walsh, I'm sure the £8k raised will be very well spent.

As promised, I've enclosed a brochure on our services and would be very happy to talk these through with you when you've got over your hectic spell on the new product launch.

In the meantime I hope you and your family have a great holiday in France. Based on our experience of a couple of years ago, I'm sure your girls will love it. I'll make a note to give you a call when you've had time to settle back into business after your break.

Yours

Jackie Channon

To me, that letter said 'professional, not too pushy, personable and different' – the sort of contact from whom you would welcome the follow-up call. Naturally, when she phoned, Jackie would have pulled out my card and details, together with her letter, and have been in a great position to ask about my holiday, how the new product launch was going and if I'd managed to get my desk back in order following my break.

In the ebb and flow of conversation Jackie would also have picked up that as a result of my family's visit to France I've now become interested in wines and she would have made a note of that as a potential gift or invitation should I become a valued client or contact.

You can almost picture the follow-up letter four months later at Christmas:

> Thanks for your business, it really is appreciated. I thought you might like to try this new French Chardonnay which one of my other clients has just started importing.
>
> If you like it I'll introduce you to him, or perhaps you and your wife may like to attend one of his wine-tasting evenings. Let me know what you think when you have a minute.

This is what I call the 'sophisticated' client relationship. Based on a couple of snippets of information, Jackie has not only provided a token (the wine only cost £6 a bottle) but also a very relevant gift. She is also helping another of her clients, the wine importer, in a very 'soft sell' way to be introduced to a potential new customer – a 'win–win' situation all round.

Write it down

So that's the reason why you should capture information from the people you talk to on the back of their card – it's professional and it's the glue that helps you to build relationships and business.

The alternative – to do nothing and hope you remember – is no alternative at all, because you probably won't. More than once I've received literature or a phone call from a contact I'd met recently who had confused me with someone else at the same event. This was embarrassing for them and their 'street cred' rating with me was, of course, zero!

TRY THIS

Take a card at random out of your contacts system, wallet or wherever you keep other people's cards. Try to recall as much as you can about the person, your last conversation, their likes and dislikes and your next action with them.

Would this exercise have been easier if you'd jotted down a few notes on the back of the card?

Take the banker's approach

If writing on the back of cards appears somewhat 'tacky' to you (and I can understand your point of view), take a leaf out of the book of a banker I met recently. He carried with him a tiny silver-cased notepad not much larger than a business card and when we had agreed a mutual action he went through the same routine as for the cards and asked my permission by saying: 'My memory is not as good as it once was [bet it is]. Would you mind if I just captured that action?' Then he produced his silver-cased pad and its associated tiny silver pen and proceeded to write my name and what we'd agreed to do on the next clean sheet. Very professional and sophisticated – and he did indeed follow up. I assume that he captured the other details I told him during our conversation on my card later.

Soak up the basics in seconds

Anyway, back to what *you* do with other people's business cards when you receive them. The first thing you should do with a card is to *read* it. Not only is it good manners, but reading the card will also help 'fix' the key details in your memory. It only takes a few seconds to scan your conversation partner's name, title, organisation and its location, and any other information on the card, and doing so gives you a wealth of conversation ammunition, for example:

- How many people have you got in Birmingham (or wherever)?

- Is Birmingham your head office?

- Do you have other locations around the UK or overseas?

- I see you are in surveying.
  - What does that involve?
  - What size of client do you service?
  - Who are your competitors?
  - How long has your business been established?

- Have you been at the Centre Business Park long?
  - How do you like it as a business location?
  - What other businesses are there at the Park?

- Have you been with XYZ Consultants long?
  - Have you always been in this specialist area?
  - Where were you before?
  - What training do you need for your specialism?

TRY THIS

Pull out any card from your contacts file and take a few seconds to look at it. Then consider what questions you would have at your disposal when conversing with that person.

You can see that from a cursory glance at someone's business card it is entirely possible to have an interesting and in-depth conversation in a number of areas. That's why top connectors *read* contacts' cards when they are given to them. It gives them a conversation edge.

There are many more questions, depending on the circumstances, which you might ask to get the conversation flowing and find out a little more about your conversation partner. So, don't show your naivety as a networker by immediately putting the card you've just been handed into your pocket and then start asking: 'What business are you in? Where are you located? What's your role in the business?' You would have picked up all this information in five seconds if you had read the card. It's the difference between acting like a serious 'player' and looking like an amateur.

Keep your promises

OK, so you've read the card, possibly jotted down some notes on the back of it, and carried out the actions you said you would perform. I've taken it as read that you *will* do whatever you promised, not only because it makes good business sense, but also for one very personal reason: hardly anything is as embarrassing as meeting your conversation partner again at a later date (another function, perhaps) and not having done what you promised. If you don't physically start shrinking when your eyes meet theirs, your confidence and credibility will. It doesn't matter whether the action was a large or trivial one. You said you would do something and it's not been done – and that makes you look unprofessional, disorganised, lazy, uninterested or all of them rolled together. You can make your excuses, of course, but the damage has been done. Why would they trust you again?

Not doing the things you agreed to do for others is social suicide and no one is to blame except yourself. So, please, do what the ace connectors do and ensure that you act on your promises as soon as possible. Not keeping them destroys your reputation, but keeping them quickly and effectively builds it out of all proportion to the action.

IN PRACTICE

Sean Mahon, chairman of a UK-based quoted company, built his reputation as a connector, and as someone who *always* delivered on his promises, in a very simple but incredibly powerful way.

When planning his diary he would book the first hour of the day following a corporate or networking function as a 'meeting with himself'. He would arrive at the office with pockets full of business cards (with his notes on the reverse) from people he had met the previous evening and agreed an action with.

Sean would then spend the next hour – totally uninterrupted –

writing thank you letters to the host and notes to other appropriate contacts. Then he'd focus on the cards and for each in turn he'd make the appropriate response – a fast and effective way of being seen as a great connector who delivers on his promises.

CHAPTER 2

Creating a Powerful Presence

WATCH SUCCESSFUL CONNECTORS talking to those around them. They appear to know instinctively how to handle themselves and their interaction with others, and you can almost feel the respect they command. But how do they do it and what makes them so attractive?

Top connectors have figured out what works and what doesn't when dealing with people. They know that every word they say and every move they make sends a subliminal – but immensely powerful – message about them. Just as David Attenborough and his other cohorts have analysed the behaviour patterns of animals, so Dr Desmond Morris, Alan Pease and others have analysed the human species. You'll find their key discoveries sprinkled liberally throughout this chapter.

Research by psychology and body language experts has shown that many successful people have a natural ability to get people to like and appreciate them very quickly. They make people feel comfortable and safe and show an interest in them. Their whole demeanour makes them attract people like a magnet. They have 'presence'.

Those with presence exude positive energy. They look alive and interested. They command space by their confident and self-assured approach. But presence is more than just these things. You can 'feel' someone's presence in their voice too.

You develop presence when you have the right posture, attitude and body language. Let's focus on enhancing the 'essential you' and developing your 'presence rating'.

Presence, and How to Cultivate It

We'd all love to have that almost mystical power of presence. You can develop it if you are willing to work at it. But don't confuse it with charisma. People with charisma have achieved a special way of being that seems to permeate both them and the room. Some lucky folk are born with it, but for others, their life achievements and tribulations help to create it. Presence, on the other hand, is all about space and how you use it. To explain:

IN PRACTICE

In her seminars, confidence guru Meribeth Bunch asks delegates: 'How much space are you occupying just now?' The vast majority reply with something like 'Just around my chair', 'A direct line to you' or 'As far as the person sitting next to me.' She then asks them to assess the amount of space she is occupying. The usual response is: 'The whole room.'

'How do you know?' she will say. The answers include: 'Something about your posture', 'You are standing and we are sitting' and 'You are in charge of this seminar.' The delegates *know* when someone is commanding space, yet can't quite put their finger on the specific reasons why.

Your own personal space is an invisible energy field you create around yourself, and if those around you can sense it, it must be more than just imagination. The obvious indicators of your 'presence rating' are your posture, energy, eyes, voice and smile. But there's more – factors such as your attitude, thoughts and imagination also have a big say in your overall presence. By putting each of your presence ingredients under the microscope we can identify ways in which you can develop more of it. Here's secret number one:

Taking posture lessons from cats

Your posture can make or break your ability to have presence. Get it right and it helps you to look energetic, adds to your voice quality and forges the kind of image you want to project. Remember, though, that your posture is dynamic, not static. Instead of something rigid or fixed, think of yourself as being as mobile as a cat. Just this thought alone will help you to develop the right feeling of movement and power. Connectors with this kind of energy have sparkling eyes and look vibrant – just the sort of person you would want to know better.

IN PRACTICE

In a study of 10,000 people by UCLA, each respondent was asked their initial impressions of someone they later bought something from. The results may blow your mind! Seven per cent said the person had a good knowledge of their product, service or topic. Thirty-eight per cent said the person had good voice quality and sounded intelligent, confident and interested. But here's the shocker: 55 per cent said it was the way the person walked! They had an air of confidence and self-assurance, even before they said a word. How about that for the power of body language!

If the way you hold yourself can make an impact on that most tangible of measures, sales figures, you can bet that there is really something in it. The problem is that you've probably been standing, sitting and moving in the same way for years. How do you improve? The answer is gradually – but it's worth the wait.

Proponents of posture-enhancing disciplines like Pilates and the Alexander Technique can tell amazing stories of the difference the techniques have made to their own well-being and that of their pupils – not just physical enhancements, but mental and spiritual ones too. Could posture be *the* key determinant of presence? Looking at those who take the Pilates and Alexander principles to heart I would say that they are not far wrong. But before you join up for the next course...

TRY THIS

Face a mirror and put the palm of your hand just above the crown (towards the back) of your head. Looking straight ahead and keeping loose, stretch upwards with your crown to touch your hand. If you've done it correctly you'll feel quite tall and the back of your neck will be stretched and feel long. If you mistakenly place your hand at the very top and centre of your head and stretch, your chin will rise. That is not what you want.

After doing this a few times, just placing your hand over the crown will remind you to stand taller. Do it at any time when you are standing or sitting. As a reminder to stand tall, place Post-it notes on your mirrors and your desk and by your phone, where they will act as a reminder. See and feel the difference in a week.

So back to those key tips for developing presence...

Allowing the real you to shine through

Few personal attributes are more attractive than shining, sparkling eyes. They are the 'window to the soul' and an indisputable guide to your interest in what's going on. For centuries eyes have been used by doctors to diagnose illness and they are giving away what you are thinking right now.

Watch someone who is self-conscious – no doubt their eyes are not really focused on what's going on. They are preoccupied. When you are 'self-centred' in this way you prevent yourself from being fully present and it shows in your eyes. What you need to do to develop presence is to release your self-centred eyes by using 'peripheral vision'.

TRY THIS

Peripheral vision involves using a broad scope of seeing, and using 180 degree vision. Most of us are physically capable of achieving nearly 180 degrees of vision. You can test this for yourself by extending your arms to the front with your hands touching. While looking straight ahead, move your arms slowly apart, keeping them at shoulder level. Note the point when you can no longer see both hands. It is probably close to 180 degrees.

Without moving your head you can see the ceiling, the floor, everything within the 180 degrees in detail. You are seeing the context of the whole. When you look at another person this way, you see the person in front of you and most of the adjacent surroundings at the same time. This is very different to intensely glaring into their eyes and being unaware of what else may be in your space. Instead, you are visually aware of the whole scene and your eyes have a softer, less aggressive look as a result.

How you 'see' people is vital to the way you are perceived by them and is an indication of the way you manage your personal space. When you use a wide peripheral vision to see another person they know you have given them a very strong form of acknowledgement. No one likes to feel ignored. Having 'tunnel' vision when around people, whether it is simply a bad habit or deliberate, is usually interpreted as being cold, aloof and uncaring. Everyone needs acknowledgement and really 'seeing' them is the easiest way to show it.

'We have contact!'

Social scientists have proved that strong eye contact gives you the impression of being an intelligent and abstract thinker, and that exaggerated eye contact can be advantageous if used carefully.

Recent research in the United States asked people to have a casual conversation with a member of the opposite sex for two minutes. Unbeknown to the female participants, half of the male subjects were briefed in advance to have intense eye contact with their female conversation partner and were told to do this by simply counting the number of times their partner blinked during the conversation. The remainder of the men were told just to do what they would normally do.

Questioned later, the unsuspecting female blinkers reported significantly higher feelings of respect and fondness for those men who had simply been counting their blinks than the control group who had talked normally. Why? Because the blink counters appeared to be more interested in what the women were saying and demonstrated it with their body language and attention.

IN PRACTICE

There are different approaches to eye contact depending on the networking situation you find yourself in.

Imagine an inverted triangle on your face, the base of it just above your eyes and the other two sides emanating from it and coming to a point between your nose and your lips. This is the area to focus on for business conversations.

In convivial social situations, the point of the triangle drops to include the chin and neck areas.

The triangle is a way of letting your gaze rest in the vicinity of the face and ensuring that you won't be fixated on someone's eyes. One helpful hint here is to look at one eye, then both, then one eye again, rather than stare into both eyes non-stop.

Social studies suggest that looking at people's 'eye area' for about 80–90 per cent of the time you converse is the right amount. Any less and you fail to make the full impact of your connection, and any longer and you may be considered too aggressive and direct.

If you want people to like you and gain empathy with them, use the 80 per cent guide. Naturally you'll be looking at your contact when you introduce yourself, shake hands and start speaking. Equally important for cementing the relationship is holding direct eye contact when you are saying your goodbyes. It leaves your conversation partner with a strong and lasting message that you enjoyed speaking with them.

'I love it here . . .'

You've seen people who just don't want to be where they are right now. They look either distinctly uncomfortable (for example when they've got a speech to make and they would rather be *anywhere* than in front of all those people) or bored – and it shows in their uninterested body language, their glances to other parts of the room or the glazed look in their eyes. We've all done it, so don't pretend you don't know the feeling!

Contrast that with the positive alertness, interest and, yes, excitement you show when you are in situations you really enjoy and with people you really like. Capture that feeling in your mind's eye. That's the look and demeanour of someone with presence – they want to be *exactly where they are*. Right now there's no other place they'd rather be than talking to you. Does that not make you feel good? Wanting to be where you are is a prerequisite of presence.

TRY THIS

'Long Time No See'

Think of the next new contact you meet as an old friend who you used to know fantastically well when you were younger but have lost touch with over the years. Now the occasion has bought you together again.

Close your eyes and feel the sensation for a minute. What changes do you feel in your body, your face, your general attitude to the situation? You'll find that your face softens, your body language opens up and you are generally much more responsive to having a great conversation. What's more, you've got that feeling that life is good. You're eager to find out more about the other person and to share experiences.

This exercise can be an attitude-changing experience for some people and it can have a tremendous impact on how they view their conversations with strangers. They literally visualise the person in front of them as a 'long time no see' friend and the visualisation helps them to come over as a much warmer person. Don't worry, you won't go 'over the top' and treat the person as a genuine long-lost friend but, who knows, your openness might be a start of a mutually beneficial friendship or business relationship!

Just as a reverse experiment, try picturing the person you met as someone who used to bully you at school or make fun of you in some way. Now what does your body language and attitude tell you about your likely success in building rapport with this person?

Upping your voice tempo and using all the notes

Without a doubt your voice is the carrier of your presence, energy, feelings, enthusiasm and imagination, and your accent tells the unspoken story of your roots. But why can some people come over as fascinating and intelligent individuals you can listen to all day long and others sound as dull as dishwater?

The secret is one that actors are particularly familiar with. Self-awareness is part of the answer, as is the ability to let yourself go and leave your inhibitions behind. To give their voice more variety and sound more interesting, many people have to go over the top by a huge amount. It's one of the first things budding performers learn, though they may only really believe it when they see or hear themselves, on video for example.

At first 'going over the top' means taking what seems like a huge risk, and this is where a bit of courage is needed. But, surprisingly, most people find that it's really hard to exaggerate *too* much!

TRY THIS

Here's a way that Meribeth Bunch, the confidence-boosting guru, uses to help her students to work on their expressiveness.

Choose a children's story to read aloud and let yourself become completely involved in it. If you feel embarrassed, close the door. Give yourself permission to be a fool or a clown momentarily. Read the story three times, each time a little differently:

1. Read two or three minutes of the text in the way you might read to children and record yourself on video or tape recorder.

2. Read another two or three minutes of text but this time give each of the characters an appropriate voice. When no characters have dialogue, emphasise important or colourful words.

3. Next read the text and act it out at the same time. Pretend your audience is deaf and you must show them the story. This means that if the text reads 'They walked down a very long road', you demonstrate this with your hand at the same time by 'walking' with your fingers. You will feel much like a small children's entertainer, but keep going! While you are busy carrying out this ridiculous exercise, your voice will be gaining colour, giving each word its true meaning, and your pace will fit with the text rather than having the same pitch and rhythm throughout.

4. Now find a company report or newspaper and read this in the same way as you did the final version of the children's story. Beware of reverting to type! The words can be just as colourful in your report or news-clipping reading as they were for the story.

With practice you'll develop a fresh approach to your delivery, with a spontaneous rhythm and sensitivity to the words, the right pace and pauses, and you'll add to the range and colour of your voice. You'll be able to tap into your natural energy when you need to express yourself.

IN PRACTICE

If you don't believe in all of this energy field and presence stuff, consider the findings of this experiment. Dr Bernard Grad, a researcher at Canada's McGill University, conducted a unique experiment with, of all things, barley seeds.

Grad asked a well-known faith healer to hold one of two identical glass containers of salted water in his hands. Half a batch of barley seeds was watered with this 'healing water' the other with the untreated water. The seeds were then potted and left to sprout. Seven weeks later, the 'healed' seeds were not only bigger, but greener too. The experiment was repeated several times with the same effect.

Interestingly, in a variation of Grad's seed experiments, he asked a person suffering from severe depression to hold one of the water containers. Seeds watered from this container failed to grow. The message? Your energy field has the potential to have a hidden but very real effect on your environment.

So, you've established your presence. Next you need to build some rapport with those who are important to you.

CHAPTER 3

How to Build Rapport

YOUR RELATIONSHIPS ARE fundamental to your success, and since most successful people have built strong and lasting relationships with their network of key contacts, there must be some correlation between their ability to get on with people and their success. Put simply, if you have the ability to generate rapport with others, you'll be happy and successful; if you don't, you won't. Without rapport in your networking, you'll just be going through the motions and meeting lots of people who don't particularly feel an affinity with you. That's not an effective networking (or life) strategy.

Leaders in all walks of life recognise that other people are the most valuable resource they have. Charismatic leaders who demonstrate that they understand their people and their needs are often idolised by their followers. And that's where one of Steven Covey's *Seven Habits of Highly Effective People* introduces itself. 'First seek to understand, then to be understood,' he says, powerfully demonstrating that to be effective (in this case an effective networker) you need to gain information, to understand your contact's point of view and to appreciate them and their situation before launching into what's important to you.

How you build rapport is easy once you know how. But

before we get into the 'nitty gritty', let's take a look at the two types of rapport we all need to create.

The first, 'instant rapport', is the type of feeling you get when you meet someone for the first time. At its extreme this is 'love at first sight', an overpowering mutual feeling that this person is your soul-mate and understands you completely. Less passionate but equally heart-warming is the feeling you get when you meet someone and 'hit it off' immediately.

The second type of rapport is long term – like lifelong friends, buddies you only see now and again but who can pick up where you left off just as soon as you speak to them. This type of rapport is based on mutual respect and trust, sincerity, shared experiences and common interests.

Both types of rapport are super-important to a connector. It's very hard to develop long-term rapport if you've started off on the wrong foot and not built it at the 'instant' stage. Equally, the attraction of the initial rapport you create with someone pales significantly if they lose credibility by constantly letting you down, fail to deliver on their promises or lose interest in being with you. Into this category tumble lots of relationships, personal or business, where, for whatever reason, the two parties have fallen out of rapport. You may even be in conflict and one or both of you is paying the price in hurt feelings. And battered emotions, socially or in business, are not a steady platform upon which to build anything.

How a Relationship Develops

Before we get into the specifics of how to create rapport, check out this simple framework which explains how a relationship develops. It helps to set the rapport-building techniques in context. It works for business relationships but, as you read, why not reflect on your other relationships? You'll really see that the model applies there too.

The relationship triangle

The triangle shows how a relationship begins with acknowledgement and progresses through to the higher levels when we like someone, and they like us, and we bond with them. To you and me that means we become friends, or more. Let's have a look at how it all fits together.

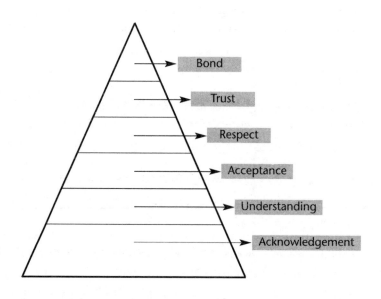

Acknowledgement

Acknowledgement is what happens when two people meet for the first time. Without acknowledgement you're not going to get far at all. After all, it's hard to forge a relationship with someone if they haven't noticed you!

When you meet someone for the first time you may exchange a few words or simply make eye contact with the other person, but what you'll really be doing is weighing each other up. An unconscious process it may be, but its effects are mighty powerful. You've probably had the experience of taking an instant like or dislike to someone, and if your instant reaction was dislike, it's very likely that you aborted the fledgling relationship right there.

Understanding

When you start to gather information about each other through conversation you begin to understand more about the other person and form an impression of them. Funnily enough, this may bear no resemblance to the truth.

On meeting Peter for the first time, for example, your observations might be that he:

- Is well groomed.

- Smiles enthusiastically.

- Gives a warm handshake.

- Talks confidently about his business.

- Dresses well.

- Is a family man.

But for all you know Peter could be a mass murderer. The point is that all of our relationships are based on the impressions we form of others. Opinions may change as people get to know each other, but early impressions often dictate how the relationship will develop.

This fact has great implications for the early stages of your relationships. Keep an open mind and try not to fall into the trap of judging others too soon. Many opportunities have been lost because a person wrongly thought their new contact was inflexible, not really interested or not ready to make a decision. Take a tip from those who have bitter experience and don't form an opinion without hard evidence.

Acceptance

Based on what impressions have been formed so far, you and your contact may decide that you want to develop the relationship. This is a joint decision, often made unconsciously, but in the business arena it sometimes takes the form of a formal agreement, like being included on a tender list or a shortlist for a contract.

The three stages of the relationship we've explored so far – acknowledgement, understanding and acceptance – are what the psychologists call the 'lower' levels. As you would expect, they are the building-blocks of the higher stages: respect, trust and bond. Let's go higher.

Respect

Now emotional ties are starting to be created. There's mutual respect and a real shift to seeing your contact in a distinctly positive light. Both of you recognise that you have things to bring to the relationship.

Trust

Trust happens when you increase your level of commitment to each other. It's when each of you feels confident that the other will deliver what is required of them and, should difficulties arise, they will be dealt with openly and with a genuine desire to resolve them. When trust is present, the other person will have total confidence that you and your organisation will act in their best interests.

Bond

In some relationships the bonds which begin to form in the respect stage develop into feelings of real affinity with the other person. Each person gives and takes at an emotional level and the relationship is now dramatically strengthened by the bonds that have formed, as well as by the business or social reasons that originally brought them together.

This is the height of the relationship and is what connectors aspire to. They know that the bond of real friendship, based on mutual respect and trust, is almost unbreakable.

TRY THIS

Think of some of your business and social relationships and plot them against these stages.

What do the results tell you about where you stand now, and what you might do in the future to build on those relationships you wish to take to higher levels?

The 16 Steps to Developing Great Rapport

Creating great rapport is about helping people who meet you for the first time to think that it is to their benefit! In short, they must immediately see some benefit from investing their time with you. You need to maximise those first few minutes, so that you can use that time as a springboard to develop a longer-term relationship.

When you meet people your main aim should be to have them relax with you. No one is fully involved in networking or making 'commitment' decisions when they are uptight or unsure. You need your contacts to like and trust you because if they don't they won't maintain the relationship and certainly won't do business with you if they can help it.

Champion connectors know they need to cover the 16 bases in this section when meeting people. Handle them well and the door will be open to a mutually beneficial relationship. Handle them badly and the door may be well and truly locked.

Think about this for starters: you have, at most, 15 seconds to make a fabulous first impression – and first impressions stick. We live in a world where we have information bombarding us all the time, so we must form quick judgements. Arguably, it's always been like that. The caveman had 15 seconds to decide whether the animal he was facing was his supper or whether he was its intended feast. Snap decisions on 'fight or flight' were the order of the day long ago!

Now, just as then, we take a mental snapshot of the situation in front of us and act accordingly. Do we like the look of this person? For the connector the answer has to be 'yes' or they will have real difficulty in building rapport with their conversation partner. Think of a 'no' as starting a 100-metre race 10 yards further back than the rest of the competitors – it's going to be hard work and your chances of success are slim. Get on the right track straight away by doing this:

1. Smile!

A smile shows that you are warm, open and friendly. A poker face, rightly or wrongly, sends out the signal that you are definitely serious and possibly cold and unapproachable. A smile carries your personality with it, lights up your face and puts a sparkle in your eye. Use it to say 'I'm really happy to see you' even before you've opened your mouth. They say a picture is worth a thousand words – so is a smile to a connector.

Think of a 'flirting' smile. You look, then you smile, broad and warm, not a silly grin. If you don't like that allegory, think of the sun coming out from behind a cloud, gathering in intensity and warmth as it moves out into the open.

But beware of the danger of smiling too much, too often. The idea is to create a special smile for the unique person in front of you, not an automatic grin for everyone you see. A fixed smile for all will be perceived as false, even if it's genuinely meant – a poor politician's tactic.

2. Put them in the spotlight

Every good connector knows that the secret of getting people to like you is to show how much you are interested in them. Dale Carnegie highlighted this message in his 1936 bestseller *How to Win Friends and Influence People* and it's been used ever since by those who know that focusing on others, not themselves, is the secret of success.

For most people, however, the problem is that we get overtaken by self-consciousness and spend too much time thinking about what impression we are making and what we 'should' be doing next, instead of reacting spontaneously and naturally to the other person in the way we do when we are with someone we feel very comfortable with.

3. 'Matchmaker, matchmaker, make me a match'

Not everyone under pensionable age will remember the classic song from the film *Fiddler on the Roof* imploring the village's matchmaker (who found wives for lovelorn bachelors) to help, but the technique holds true.

The matchmaker analysed the physical and personality traits of the gentleman in question and found a compatible partner – a 'match'. Social psychologists have done the same. While they may not be able to belt out a song quite like the cast of the film, they can give us some great advice on building good feelings between people. It goes like this: match the posture and rhythm of the person you want to gain rapport with, and then watch what happens.

We're talking here about listening and observing, matching their energy but not mimicking. It's about broadly 'mirroring' someone's general posture, speech and tone of voice; talking the language they are familiar with and using the words they would use. It's even about getting in step with the rhythm of their breathing. This is by no means as far-fetched as it sounds. Therapists have been using the technique for years to help their patients feel close to them.

But the next stage is where the therapists really turn it on. After a short while 'mirroring' and getting in tune with their contact's mood, they then 'lead' them with their own body language and pace, moving them from a negative frame of mind and closed posture to a more open and receptive one. It works!

Make no mistake; we're not talking here about a gimmick to trick your contact into believing you are interested in them when you are not. When you are genuinely interested in someone and sensitive to their needs you do naturally fall into body and voice tone alignment.

Look at lovers in a restaurant – the tell-tale 'mirrored' body language, eye contact and pace of speech usually give them away, even if they are trying to hide it. If you observe closely enough you may even see them pick up their drinks at the same time or just seconds after each other.

No one who is down ever appreciates an insensitive 'Cheer up, it may never happen' comment. But they usually welcome a sympathetic 'You look a bit down... Is there anything I can do to help?' The time for the coach's slap on the back and pep talk comes later, once rapport is established. Connectors know that they need to mirror others before bringing them up to their speed.

Knowing the positive effects of matching people's mood and movement is one of the real secrets of instant rapport. Use it wisely and mirror, don't copy. You may have played a game when you were a child, or even as an adult if you've still some fun left in you, where you copied everything your pal did and repeated everything they said. Do you remember how mad they got and how irritated you yourself felt when they did it to you? Matching should be subtle, not blatant, and should be employed with the aim of meeting your contact's needs, not manipulating them.

IN PRACTICE

Mirroring can be done consciously in a business situation. David Lewis, author of *The Secret Language of Success*, has found that mirroring increases the chances of agreement by up to 50 per cent during negotiations and doubles your chances of making a favourable impression during sales presentations.

4. Are you in or out?

Top connectors have developed a 'nose' for whether they are in or out of rapport with someone. They've heightened their sensitivity to both the obvious and more subtle signs of what people say, the way they say it and how they hold themselves. It's more than recognising a rebuff when asking for a date; it's about reading between the lines of body language to see what people are really thinking.

What's the red light which warns you that you haven't got rapport with someone? Simple – you'll be acting and thinking differently from them.

TRY THIS

Try this little social interaction experiment with someone you know well and have a good rapport with – your partner, a work colleague or a friend, for example.

Get into a normal conversation with them (which means that you're very likely to be in rapport) and then after a short while deliberately try to get out of rapport. Unsynchronise your body language by changing your posture, hold their gaze for less time and look away more frequently, make your voice higher or lower, or make each pause longer or shorter. Change your mood so that it is different from theirs – be demonstrably happier or more morose.

Beware, though – if you try to do all these at once you'll look and sound like a maniac and have your friend dialling the local ambulance service. Just try one or two of these permutations and watch your rapport level sink as you both become more uncomfortable.

This is a dynamic demonstration of the building-blocks of rapport and how quickly, through lack of knowledge or inappropriate use, you can bring them tumbling down.

5. Dress to impress

This doesn't mean that you have to wear a tuxedo all the time, or even your best clothes. But the instant rapport kings recognise that to be liked by people it's important to look like them too.

It's all about 'group norms' as the social workers would call it, but a more memorable definition is 'When in Rome, do as the Romans do.' A three-piece suit might have made you stand out from the crowd in ancient Rome, but it wouldn't have been your ticket to the toga-wearing 'in crowd'.

So, if your organisation is a casual dress environment, wear casuals; if it's a formal suit place, wear a suit. I'm not suggesting that everyone should be a dress clone of everyone else but, particularly if you are meeting contacts for the first time or it's early days in your relationship, give some thought to being 'like them' in your attire – unless they dress like a tramp, of course.

6. Strive to be interested, not interesting

Some would-be rapport-builders go wrong as soon as they utter their first words because their whole attitude to the process is wrong. They think that building rapport is about impressing the other person with their innate charm and wit. The 'Aren't I a great guy?' approach is a high-risk strategy that seldom works.

The professionals take the opposite, and altogether more successful, route. They become fascinated with the other person (and most people are fascinating when you get to know them) by asking them about themselves, finding out about their family, their views, their experiences, their hopes for the future, hobbies, holidays, cars – anything, in fact, that both parties find of interest.

Seek to find out more about others and what makes them 'tick' – be interested rather than try to be interesting – and you will both enjoy the conversation. What's more, you'll be building great rapport as the other person shares information, insights and views with you; and it's less wearing on your nerves than trying to roll out your party-piece one liners again in a desperate bid to entertain.

IN PRACTICE

One person who's built a highly successful business based on these principles is Harvey MacKay, author of the bestseller *Swim with the Sharks Without Being Eaten Alive*. The book focuses on the business-building benefits of creating wonderful relationships with customers by really getting on their wavelength.

MacKay built a customer-focused attitude in his sales force by training them to learn about 66 (yes, sixty-six) aspects of their customers' personal and professional lives. His list includes finding out about obvious things like their family situation, where they go on holiday, sports, hobbies, likes and dislikes, and what they want from their suppliers, their relationships and their life.

But that's only part of the equation. MacKay also trains his people how to, appropriately, send cards, thank you's and information relevant to their goals, hobbies and ambitions. It's a mammoth exercise in building customer relations and it wins because it keeps customer relations absolutely where they should be – right at the forefront of his people's minds.

7. Size nines, slim fit

'Put yourself in their shoes' are the words our mother used to say to my brother and me whenever we were complaining about someone or something. I can hear her saying it now as I recall us bemoaning the fact that we had no electricity in the home one evening – part of a series of blackouts caused by an energy crisis in the UK in 1974 as a result of the miners' strike.

'Put yourself in their shoes,' she said. 'These people have blackouts too, but they are fighting for their jobs, their pits and the survival of their whole community.' Gulp! She changed our perspective on that transient irritation.

The point? You can't begin to build real rapport with people unless you seek to understand them, to see things through their eyes, to try to experience things the way they do.

TRY THIS

Put yourself in the shoes of your partner or a friend. Consider their role in life, what they do with their time and, in particular, the challenges they face. (If you find this difficult, maybe you are not as close as you think.) Imagine you are them. Try to 'feel' the way they do. If you've done it properly and really got into their life and mindset, it's almost certain you'll have a fresh appreciation of them as a person. You'll understand them at a much deeper level than before.

What's the implication for networkers? Observe people's mood and demeanour before you rush in. What's happening with them at that moment? Match their mood, happy or sad. Empathise with them. Then you will have earned the right to move them gently towards your mood.

8. Use names

Dale Carnegie described a person's own name as the 'sweetest sound anyone ever hears'. People pay attention when they hear their own name (think back to school), they love you when you remember it and you make them feel special when you use it.

What's the moral? Don't forget it for one thing, and make sure that you use it appropriately in conversation. Chapter 6 will give you techniques for remembering and using people's names (*see pages 141–55*).

9. You too!

You instantly feel closer to people who have something in common with you, whether it's your home town, a mutual friend, a love of the same football team, sport or hobby, the same school, the same views on, whatever. It doesn't really matter what it is, people just love to have things in common. It makes them feel safe; they are on familiar territory – and they like you for it.

The implication for connectors is obvious. Listen for areas of common interest and ask questions that will get you on the highway to common ground. Questions like 'Is that a London accent I detect?' and 'How do you spend your time when you're not at the office?' are, at the very least, great conversation developers. At a party, for example, a great way of establishing common ground with people you don't know is to ask: 'How do you know the host?' You're almost certainly onto a good topic here – unless, of course, you are talking to a gatecrasher!

10. Roll out the red carpet

For the uninitiated, 'red carpets' are traditionally used for royalty and other dignitaries as a sign of respect for their position. Making contacts feel special is an attribute of all the great connectors. That means genuinely caring about the well-being of others and observing – even stretching – the social graces in order to demonstrate that you like and respect the person with you.

The connector's red-carpet treatment takes the form of including their contact fully in the conversation, asking their views and listening attentively to their opinions. Rapport-builders make sure that their companion is comfortable, fed and watered, and administer the range of social graces appropriate to the situation and culture, from refreshing their drink to opening the door, passing the biscuits or holding the umbrella.

You already know the 101 things you could do to make your contacts feel better about knowing you and being with you. All of them add up to you saying: 'You are important to me.' Appeal to a person's need to feel special and they'll love you for it.

11. Introduce yourself with panache

The way you introduce yourself sends an instant message to your contact. The words you use and the way you deliver them speak volumes about the way you feel about yourself and your position in life.

Because this is so important I've devoted a whole section to it in a later chapter (*see page 79*). Suffice to say here that a down-beat delivery shouts 'Boring!' Self-introductions are the equivalent of surfing the radio channels for one that tickles your fancy. Based on what you hear, you decide almost immediately whether to 'tune in' or move on to the next station. It's the same with introductions. A poor one will have your contact tuning you out before you've even got started. And while they may not be rude enough to metaphorically 'change channels' and move on immediately, they'll have decided that there's something more to their taste elsewhere.

12. Deliver it warm, and with hooks

It's not what you say, it's how you say it that's important in your opening line. In fact you can say almost anything you want as an opener as long as it puts people at their ease and sounds warm and friendly. Your job here is no more than to demon-strate to them that you think that they are OK and to break down the almost inevitable feeling of subliminal fear, suspicion and mistrust (back to caveman instincts, I'm afraid).

The key message here is not to worry about your first words, since 80 per cent of your listener's first impression hasn't got any-thing to do with your words anyway. All you need is an empathic mood, a positive attitude and a warm and friendly delivery.

Like fishing with several lines at once, the best way to get your 'hooks' into a conversation from the start is to give your conversation partner plenty of bait. This means providing infor-mation about yourself so that they can follow up whichever 'line' most appeals.

13. Shake, touch or not?

Not every situation warrants a handshake, a hug, a kiss on the cheek or any kind of touch at all. You need to be guided by your own feelings at the time and the social 'norms' of the particular situation. Nevertheless, if you do shake hands there are some dos and don'ts to watch out for.

Your handshake, rightly or wrongly, telegraphs a great deal of information about you. Many potential relationships have hit the rocks before they've begun because a weak and lifeless handshake has given the impression of a weak and lifeless person.

A good firm handshake is a key aspect of building rapport. Even for women, the accepted protocol is that it's better to err on the side of firm than weak. If you go for weak, you'll be in danger of having your fingers crushed by some of the more insensitive handshakers. Go for firm!

Here are a few handshakes you'll meet in your networking travels:

- **Normal** Where the hands fit snugly together 'web to web'. Moving up and down two or three times for usually no more than three seconds, the hands themselves remain parallel and vertical, with both parties exerting the same amount of pressure.

- **Controller** Where a person extends their hand to you 'web to web' but as soon as your hands are linked, they purposely move their hand onto the top. This is a sign that they are trying to take charge. It means that you will need to be thinking a step ahead if the relationship is to go forward.

- **Dead fish** Where there's very little movement in the other person's hand. No emotion passes to you and, just like a dead fish, the hand is often clammy. All in all, you usually can't wait to remove your hand from this type of handshake.

- **Fingers only** Where only the fingers are offered and you're not exactly sure how to grasp them or how hard to shake. This is both a male and female trait, but women do it largely for fear of their hand being crushed by their male counterpart.

- **Sandwich** Where you envelop the person's hand with both of yours. Politicians often use this technique to show sincerity (watch them on the TV), but it's best used with people you know well.

- **The bone crusher** Some men haven't got the hang of how much force to use in a handshake and tend to overdo it with a vice-like grip. This is usually due to a misguided effort to have a firm handshake, or is possibly a tactic to intimidate.

IN PRACTICE

A study of the power of touch in influencing a sale generated some remarkable findings.

A group of salespeople were asked to go through their normal sales routine but told that, apart from shaking hands, they were not to touch their prospective client.

A second group was given instructions to touch the prospective client at an appropriate time on the upper arm, somewhere between the shoulder and elbow. Example situations would be when escorting them to the lift, showing them to the meeting-room or emphasising a particular point. The idea was to do it as naturally as possible as part of normal body language.

Guess what? The 'touchers' clinched significantly more (48 per cent more!) sales than those who kept their hands to themselves.

The researchers concluded a few things from the experiment, all of which are absolutely relevant to anyone who wants to build rapport. Touching a 'non-threatening' area of another person is a good way to show that you like them and feel comfortable with them. It allows you into their personal space with little risk of rejection and embarrassment and as long as it is perceived by the other as having no ulterior motive, is socially acceptable and helps build a bond.

But beware – there are only a few non-threatening areas. Shaking hands, touching the upper arm momentarily and the back at shoulder-blade height are OK. However, though you may get away with tousling your young son's hair as a sign of affection, it wouldn't have *quite* the same effect on an adult you've just met!

The researchers in the touching the arm experiment went a stage further and explored what the results would be if the salespeople touched prospective clients on their lower arm, from the elbow to the hand. They particularly observed the reaction of the people being touched. When asked afterwards, many said that they felt that their personal space had been invaded and that the action was inappropriate for the situation. Others said that they liked it and liked the other person more as a result!

Perhaps it's in the technique and how it's done, but the key message is that touch is a rapport-building technique when it's done naturally, appropriately and with absolute integrity.

14. Use space effectively

Cementing feelings of rapport has a lot to do with using your personal space correctly. We'll come on to this later in this chapter, but for now suffice it to say that we all have our own personal space bubble into which we only allow people we know and trust. If someone who doesn't fit these criteria enters, we try to back off and regain a comfortable space between ourselves and our conversation partner. You'll see this all the time in the pubs and clubs around town. Observe whether someone moves closer to or further away from their conversation partner. It's a sure sign of whether they are in rapport or not.

Body-language experts have pointed out the real importance of knowing what space does to your rapport-building efforts. When you want to show something, say a brochure or report, your best bet for successful rapport-building is to sit next to the other person. This position naturally leads to a feeling of sharing and togetherness.

When you sit opposite someone, the reverse can happen. You're eyeball to eyeball with them, a position that tends to add formality and seriousness to the situation. You have the space between you now and an invisible line drawn down the middle of it.

Doctors have now moved away from the face-to-face position to the side-on approach (*see diagram, page 68*) – because it's a halfway house between the informality of sitting next to each other and sitting directly opposite each other with the desk as a barrier between you.

Connectors know that one of the great rapport-building secrets is to align their body so that they are pointing in a similar direction to their conversation partner. As a result, they and their contacts are much more likely to view things in the same way. They are going in the same direction and they share the same space in front of them. The demarcation line doesn't exist.

TRY THIS

When you are out of rapport with someone, try aligning your body direction with theirs. Face the same way, get next to them, share the space in front of you and feel the change in atmosphere between you. It works!

We'll pick up on the connector's tactics for seating arrangements at meetings later, but here's a sneak preview.

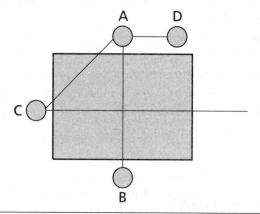

A sits opposite B: Often seen as the negotiation or 'adversarial' position. Eye to eye, with an invisible, but real, territory 'demarcation line' down the middle of the table.

C sits at 45° to A. The new doctor/patient seating arrangement. More open, less territorial, but still professional.

D sits next to A. Informal, friendly, sharing of information and perspective. Both are 'sharing' the space in front of them. Much harder to disagree from this position of closeness.

Top connectors in business recognise the need to use space to their advantage. If they have to give a formal reprimand to a work colleague or a supplier, they may think twice about sitting next to them, or even at right angles.

IN PRACTICE

One senior partner of an international law firm made a science out of using seating positions appropriately.

For formal discussions with representatives of the other party he would have them sit opposite him.

In subsequent discussions when progress was being made on particular negotiation points he reverted to the semi-formal right-angle position to lessen the potential for conflict and improve the feeling of coming closer together on a settlement.

Finally, when he'd reached the point of knowing what his offer should be and needed to persuade the other side that this was a 'win offer' for them, the meeting would be at the smaller round table in his office.

He would sit next to his professional rival to share thoughts (and common space). He'd take them through a document, highlighting points with his pen. His subliminal message was: 'We've now reached common ground, we're seeing things the same way, we are equals and, in fact, want the same things.' Now that's an intelligent, and case-winning, use of space!

15. Reveal yourself

You can only go so far in building rapport if you don't tell people anything about yourself.

The experienced connector's rule of thumb is to provide enough 'hooks' of personal information for their conversation partner to hang their own questions upon. That means matching your conversation partner's level of openness – possibly more if it's a relationship you wish to pursue (it stimulates the conversation and signals sharing) and less if you don't wish to go any deeper. All this is straightforward common sense and it usually happens automatically because people become guarded with folk they are unsure of. Nevertheless, consciously knowing what you are doing, and why, is a valuable weapon in your rapport-building armoury.

16. Listen to them

If you don't listen to what your contact has to say, you'll surely fail to develop the full level of rapport possible for the situation. Connectors have trained themselves not only to listen to the whole of what their conversation partner has to say but also to tune into the big rapport-building moments. When they hear their conversation partner start to say 'I think ...', 'I want ...' or 'My view is...', they know that good material is on its way because the person is revealing what is important to them.

Listening properly creates empathy. It says: 'You're safe here', 'I'm like you' and even 'I like you' – all without you uttering a word.

THE CONNECTOR'S TOOLKIT

Let's recap on the basic building-blocks of creating a powerful presence and building instant and long-lasting rapport.

Step 1. Stand tall
Remember the value of carrying yourself properly? Shoulders back, chest comfortably out, relaxed but confident walk, open palms...

Step 2. See
Make eye contact and remember to see your conversation partner as warm and friendly, and your eyes will soften accordingly. We don't want cold or piercing eyes here, it's not a staring contest! Eye contact is all about letting people see your friendly

personality reflected in your eyes, but there's no need to hold it for too long. A couple of seconds of solid eye contact should do the job.

Step 3. Smile

We're talking here about a warm smile, not a cheesy grin or a feeble attempt. If you don't know (or can't feel) the difference, practise your smile in the mirror. It's not as crazy as it sounds. You've probably never focused on your own smile before (after all you usually can't see your own face in normal day-to-day interaction), so give it a go and experiment with different smiles. Remember, you are after one that portrays you as friendly and approachable, not a crazed clown.

Step 4. Speak

Greet your conversation partner warmly and appropriately. Be professional, and don't be overfamiliar too soon. Your aim is to create the right impression, not engender the feeling that you are pushy or not observing the social graces. The appropriate opener may range from 'Hi' and 'Hello', to 'Good morning' or 'Good evening', depending on the context. But whatever the words, say them with a spark of enthusiasm and a distinct undertone that you are, indeed, very glad to meet the other person.

Step 5. Shake hands

Shake hands (if appropriate) properly. Not all greeting occasions warrant a handshake or hug, of course, and some people are reticent about them anyway. Play it by ear and be prepared.

If you are called on to shake hands, the correct way to do it is to grasp the whole hand of your contact and go web to web, giving it a brief but solid squeeze – neither a vice-like grip nor an impression of a wet fish. Keep it brief – too long and your contact will start to feel uncomfortable.

Step 6. Sound interesting!

Who could forget the distinctive sounds of 'Satchmo' Louis Armstrong, or Barry White, Ella Fitzgerald or Tina Turner? We've all been moved by a silky male or female voice when we've met someone for the first time; however, even the best looking of connectors can spoil their image with an unpleasant voice or dull tone.

Step 7. Question and listen

You win friends and business by understanding others and you can't do that if you don't ask the right questions and listen to what they have to say in reply. Of course you play your part in providing information to develop the conversation and the relationship, but by questioning with genuine interest and listening actively, you can't help but develop rapport. You'll control the conversation too . . . but more of that in the next chapter.

The Power of Body Language

Would you believe that the most influential pre-twentieth-century study of body language was Charles Darwin's *The Expression of the Emotions in the Man and Animals*, published in 1872?

Since then, researchers have identified nearly one million non-verbal cues and signals. Experiments by Albert Mehrabian, one of the later body-language gurus, shook traditional views of communication when he pronounced that the total impact of a message is about 7 per cent verbal (words only) and 38 per cent vocal (including tone of voice and inflection) and a staggering 55 per cent non-verbal ('body language' to you and me).

As a follow on, Professor Ray Birdwhistell calculated that the average person only speaks words for a total of about 10 or 11 minutes a day and that the average sentence takes only 2.5 seconds! Like Mehrabian he found the verbal component of a face-to-face conversation is less than 35 per cent and that over 65 per cent of communication takes place non-verbally. That's the reason why connectors have to know the body-language 'lingo' and work with it.

You may not have given it much thought up to now, but the basic body-language gestures are the same all over the world. People smile when they are happy and frown or scowl when they are angry or upset. Nodding the head is almost universally used to indicate 'yes' or affirmation. Likewise, shaking your head from side to side to indicate 'no' will be recognised by the vast bulk of the world population. It may even be a gesture that's in our genes. When a baby has had enough milk, for example, it turns its head from side to side to reject its mother's breast.

The important point for the connector is that body language is just as critical as what you say. Studying this fascinating subject ensures that the silent language of our body gives us the best opportunity to create empathy with our contacts. Ignorance, in this case, is not bliss.

Personal space

We've talked about personal space already in the context of 'presence', but there's much more to it than that. Like other animals man has his own portable personal 'space bubble' that he carries around with him. The size of yours at any given time depends on where you are, the message you are giving and to whom you are giving it. Psychologists tell us that we all have four distinct zone distances:

■ **The Intimate Zone** Between 6 and 18 inches. Only those who are emotionally close to us are allowed into this space. This includes lovers, parents, spouses, children, close friends and relatives.

■ **The Personal Zone** Between 18 and 48 inches. This is the distance we put between ourselves and others at cocktail parties, office parties, social functions and friendly gatherings.

- **The Social Zone** Between 4 and 12 feet. We stand at this distance from strangers and people we don't know very well – or don't like much.

- **The Public Zone** Anything over 12 feet. If we are talking to a large group, this is the distance at which we choose to stand. Anything closer and we feel 'hemmed in'.

Understanding gestures

We are 'speaking' all the time with our body, whether we know it or not. Our gestures reveal our innermost thoughts and are formed by a complex mixture of emotion, habit and response to particular situations. Knowledge of what gestures mean and how to react to them is, therefore, a key relationship-building skill.

We've already covered one of the critical aspects of body language – your posture. How you hold yourself says a great deal about your attitude towards the situation you find yourself in, and towards life in general. But there are many other gestures we use which have been analysed by experts who have drawn some general conclusions on what they mean.

I say 'general' for a very good reason. It's important not to jump to conclusions and interpret a single body-language gesture in isolation from others, or from what is being said. You may be right in your interpretation – but equally you could be miles off the mark and adopt the wrong response as a result.

Folding the arms, for example, is seen as a classic 'defensive' gesture by many body-language analysts, but they also concede that the arm folder could simply be in the habit of folding their arms and not feel in the least bit defensive. In fact the reason they are folding their arms could be that they are cold! So, the warning is clear: don't jump to conclusions when watching body language – look out for supporting signs to back up your 'gut feelings'.

IN PRACTICE

> Ace connectors have varied techniques for 'unlocking' those arms and moving them into a more neutral and helpful position – for example, extending their hand to shake hands if they have not done so already, or asking for a business card and offering theirs. In more formal networking situations they may share a brochure with their conversation partner or move them out of the immediate environment by suggesting a visit to the buffet table or to a publications display or exhibition stand, for example.
>
> When a contact's arms are unfolded, they tend to be more receptive. But watch out if they immediately fold their arms again – now is probably not the best time to make your 'pitch'.

Whole books have been written dissecting each and every gesture, but what should the connector look out for specifically? Here are 13 moves people make in business and social settings. I could have chosen many more. Make a mental note of what they may mean and check it out for yourself in real life. Become a 'people watcher'. Not only will it add to the quality of your interactions with people, but you'll also find yourself more interested in them because you're not only taking in the words but interpreting their 'silent' language too. These are just some of the key aspects of body language to watch out for when networking:

Eyes

Normally the top eyelid rests midway between the pupil and the iris. If it raises much above the pupil this will normally indicate extreme interest or surprise. If, on the other hand, you see your conversation partner's eyelid drop below this midpoint, they are bored, uninterested or falling asleep! If the bottom eyelid raises slightly, this normally indicates that they are evaluating what you have said, often critically. These are subtle movements, but you will easily be able to spot them if you are watching out for them.

Hand near/over mouth

This is assumed by some body-language experts to be the body's reaction to telling a lie or withholding some aspect of information. It's more than just shielding the voice in a whispering and conspiratorial manner; rather it is an involuntary action undertaken when not telling quite the full story. Newsreaders, for example, are trained to scrupulously avoid putting their hands anywhere near their face when presenting.

Legs crossed towards you

This normally indicates an interest in you or what you are saying (or it could just be the most comfortable position).

Legs crossed away from you

Normally indicates the reverse of the above (but could just be comfort again).

Ear tugging

Normally indicates evaluation or discomfort.

Tapping of pencil or other object on a desk

Could be an annoying habit, or a sign for you to get on with it!

Leaning back, hands behind head

This is interpreted as a classic sign of comfort in the situation and a 'know it all' attitude.

'Steepled' hands

Fingers joined in a loose 'prayer-like' position is interpreted as: 'I have authority and am in some way superior to you.' It is often a position adopted when people are evaluating you or what you have said.

Full body turned towards you

This is a great body-language gesture to use with people when you are greeting them. It shows that you are giving them your full attention and has a marked effect on how they react. Much better than the 'Hello' said with a glance over your shoulder!

Finger in collar

This often means the person is uncomfortable with what you have said – or just uncomfortable (particularly if the environment is hot).

Scratching the neck

Research by Desmond Morris in *The Naked Ape* concluded that telling a lie causes a tingling sensation in the delicate facial and neck tissues. A rub or a scratch is required to satisfy it. Watch out for this one – you'll see it more often than you think.

Finger on cheek

The index finger pointing up and resting on the cheek, often with the head tilted slightly, suggests that the listener finds what you are saying interesting and is evaluating it.

Open hands, palms showing

This is a 'nothing to hide' gesture taught to most salespeople. Recipients of it see the person as honest and trustworthy. Think of the gestures of priests and religious figures – the Pope, for example – a 'palms up' approach is the order of the day.

TRY THIS

Visualise in the same way that top sportspeople do. Rehearse being the person you want to be. See yourself with great posture, greeting people, shaking hands, smiling your 'sunny' smile and using a warm, steady gaze. Hear yourself chatting comfortably with everyone. Feel the pleasure of knowing you want to be there and that people like you. See yourself as someone with something unique.

The more you visualise yourself in this way the more you will 'become' that person. You'll feel increasingly comfortable with the image you have created and will behave accordingly.

Now that we've got a feel for creating presence and building rapport, let's check out the way champion connectors steer the communication in the direction they wish it to go, effortlessly and with respect.

CHAPTER 4

Communicating with Confidence

THE INTERPERSONAL SKILLS of building rapport and finding common ground are vital before launching into what you and your organisation do and what you can do for another person.

In this chapter we'll be looking at introducing yourself with confidence, using questions to develop and keep control of a discussion, and listening actively to pick up vital information. These three key skills are the foundation of developing your conversation partner's initial interest in you and demonstrating your interest in them.

Introducing Yourself with Panache

For some reason many people get tongue-tied when they are asked: 'And what do you do?' Whether it's embarrassment about their role, a lack of status they feel in their organisation ('I just work in finance') or insecurity about their ability to come over as an interesting person, many would-be networkers clam up at this point. When I run my networking courses and ask participants to answer this question, they almost invariably share these thoughts of inadequacy – as if the only role that would somehow be acceptable is one that they don't fulfil at the moment.

Your 30-second 'preview'

But the truth is that *everyone* makes a contribution – and also has the ability to encapsulate it in a 30-second 'preview', one that provides a snapshot of their personality and what they do in a lively and interesting way.

Think of it as watching those short movie previews before the big film at the cinema. They are specifically created to give you highlights of what's coming up, stir your emotions, pique your interest and make you think: 'That looks good!' That's exactly the feeling you want to create in the first few seconds with your conversation partner. It requires a bit of forward thinking if you don't want to 'shoot from the hip' because, as any gunslinger would have told you, shooting from the hip ain't as sure as a carefully aimed, pre-planned shot.

What we are looking for is a form of words that best describes you and what you do, and that you are happy with. The knack here is to find a balance between highlighting your best assets and bragging. No one likes someone who blows their own trumpet just as soon as you meet them. It sets up a prejudice barrier which is difficult to get over – first impressions are often last impressions.

At the other end of the scale, being unduly modest doesn't help either. Hiding your light under a bushel isn't a great relationship-building platform. It's the equivalent of that movie preview voiceover saying, 'This is an average film, with a predictable plot and featuring nondescript actors you've not heard of.' Does that make you say: 'Wow, this is a must see'? Unfortunately, too may people fall into this 'B' film category when introducing themselves.

We can't all be international playboys or girls, saviours of the world or lion tamers – but we can be ourselves, and we can learn to focus not just on what we do, but the benefits of what we do. How do we go about it?

Don't be bald

A bald statement is a 'B' film approach. Never just say 'I'm a pilot/doctor/dentist/surveyor/nurse/whatever.' Why? Although it provides a label, it gives your conversation partner no hooks to get their conversational 'teeth' into. They'll need to probe for more information – and many don't.

Bring what you do to life by adding some colour and personality. The pilot would find it better to say: 'I fly transport aircraft taking pharmaceuticals to various destinations in the UK and Europe' and the doctor could say: 'I'm a general practitioner and have a little surgery with 2,000 patients on the outskirts of San Francisco.'

The secret to stimulating introductions is to add some meat for the conversationalist to bite on. Create a 'mind picture' of what you do, not just a label. Say a bit about what you are doing right now. In my case I could say: 'I'm a marketing director with PricewaterhouseCoopers. We're the largest professional services firm in the world now. I help the specialist accountants, tax people and other business consultants to win new work.'

People are much more likely to ask questions about what you do if you give them something of interest first. Leave the plain 'I do' for your wedding day.

Focus on how you help others

People relate more to statements that involve helping other people, because you immediately flag up the benefits of what you do. Focusing on how you help others usually brings out the hidden side of your job – and most jobs have one.

Tune into their wavelength

It's important to recognise the nature of your audience and tailor your preview appropriately. A good preview will include your name and something about yourself that establishes what you have in common with other people in the situation you find yourself in. Like the best film previews, keep it short, punchy and interesting – you're not giving your life story or the opening lines of the Gettysburg Address.

Context is important. If I were at a wedding, for example, I'd come over far better by saying 'Hello, I'm John Timperley, an old schoolfriend of the bridegroom' than by giving my job role. If, on the other hand, I found myself at a local chamber of commerce function and was speaking to the owner of a small company, I might say: 'I'm a marketing director with PricewaterhouseCoopers. We're the biggest firm in the *region* now. My job is to ...'

Think about how your conversation partner is likely to react to what you say. In this case saying that we are the biggest firm in the region (which is true) is likely to be more relevant than saying we are the biggest in the world. My conversation partner's business is local, so I must think local and make my comments relevant. Now if I were talking to a representative of Microsoft, Sony, Hewlett Packard or any of the other global players, the story would be different.

Create and edit your own 30-second preview

The key points of your commercial can include various elements. Think about:

- The role you have in life.

- The job you do.

- What projects you are involved with right now.

- How you help others by your actions.

- Your hobbies, interests, passions.

- What you have done in the past.

- What you plan to do in the future.

- The benefits you bring to people.

The answers to these questions will open the door to your personality and the things you may want to share with people when you meet them. They will also give you the flexibility you need for different social situations. Clearly you wouldn't launch straight into your goals and vision for the future in the first half minute of meeting someone, but just knowing what your vision for the future is will help you to say the right thing when asked, and the same applies to any of the other questions above.

TRY THIS

Embarrassing as it may seem, the only real way to be very comfortable with your various 30-second openers is to practise by saying them out loud to yourself. It doesn't matter a jot if you sound awful, get your words mixed up or generally feel silly. If you persevere, you'll very quickly find that all of a sudden you become very comfortable with the sound of your own voice talking about yourself in a lively and interesting way.

Each time you do this you'll be chipping away at your 'comfort zone' and the inbuilt reticence most of us have about 'promoting' ourselves. After a while, when you are asked: 'And what do you do?', you'll find the words simply tripping off your tongue. Try it – it works!

Asking the Right Questions

If there is one face-to-face communication technique that sets top connectors apart from the crowd, it's the questions they ask and the way they ask them. They phrase their questions carefully to ensure the answers they get are useful.

As children we are fascinated by the world around us and have a fantastic capacity to ask questions. Unfortunately as we grow older this often becomes reversed and the habit of talking sets in. Getting back to your childlike tendencies is not difficult if you know how and can have the fantastic advantage of show-ing that you are astute and, most important of all, interested. Here's why:

- **Asking questions is heavily dependent on listening** If you don't pay attention to what's being said, you can't ask perti-nent questions.

- **Questions invite others to connect with you** intellectually and emotionally, and can often dig up opportunities and potential problems.

- **Being interested in the speaker flatters them** while giving strong signals that you trust and respect them.

- **Questions can be used as a 'safety valve' to release tension,** avoid misunderstanding and slice through defensiveness.

- **Questions can jar people into taking notice of what is going on** Remember daydreaming at school and suddenly being jolted back into the real world when the teacher asked you a direct question?

Connectors think of questions as 'landing lights' to work towards what matters. They ask questions such as 'Why?', 'What else?' and 'What then?' They probe for specifics but avoid any sense of interrogation. Where the meaning of an answer is unclear, they rephrase the query as often as is necessary to achieve a solid understanding. For example, if they don't get a clear enough answer from the question 'How can you get more business?', they may try 'If you got more business what would happen?' or 'What would you do to get more business?' The dif-ferent facets of the question will give the connector a more thorough and 'rounded' answer.

Let's take a look at some of the types of question you can ask to build rapport, show interest and obtain the information you need if you are to help your conversation partner.

Open questions: 'How do you feel...?'

Open questions are those to which it is difficult to reply with 'yes' or 'no'. They encourage the other person to divulge information. They also show that you are interested in them and their perspective. Any question starting with 'who', 'what', 'why', 'where', 'when' or 'how' will usually elicit a good answer, or at least some information which prompts a follow-up question.

Here are a few for starters:

- How do you feel about...?

- What was your view on...?

- How do you manage to...?

- Where did you...?

- What do you think about...?

- Who do you know here?

- When did you arrive?

But asking open questions isn't enough – you also have to 'reward' your conversation partner for giving you valuable information by:

- Thanking them: 'That's very interesting, thank you.'

- Praising them: 'You're very generous. Thanks for sharing that with me.'

- Smiling and making eye contact.

- Nodding.

- Agreeing with what they've said.

- Paraphrasing, to show that you are listening.

- Asking for further information: 'That's very interesting. Could you tell me a little more about that?'

- Maintaining an alert and interested posture.

- Asking follow-up questions.

Reflective questions: 'Tell me more...?'

'Reflectives' send the other person's words back to them. They are a natural follow up to open questions where, having stimulated the other person to talk, you want to go deeper. The reflective question helps them to focus on the point that interests you and yields more information.

By reflecting someone's words back to them, you encourage them to think about a problem, for example, and articulate their own solution. In this way your contact is more likely to be committed to the solution and doesn't feel insecure or suspicious.

Try these for size:

- Why is this a particular problem for you?

- Why is that important at the moment?

- What have you tried previously to achieve the results you're looking for?

- What would be your ideal solution?

When the connector has all the information they need, they'll turn up the control mechanism another notch by asking 'closed' questions like:

- Do you have a budget for this initiative?

- Is your objective to reduce down time by 20 per cent?

Even when the connector is doing most of the talking, they can keep their conversation partner's attention by asking 'test' questions which also serve to make sure that their thoughts are in line with their contact's. They'll say:

- Have I made it clear how [new idea, product, service] will solve your problem?

- Does what I've said help?

- Does it sound/look/feel right to you?

When the connector hits an objection, they'll cover it using obstacle-handling questions like:

- Yes, you're right, it does sound difficult, but if I can show you how to overcome it, will we be able to make progress?

- Is that your major/only concern?

Hypothetical questions: 'What if...?

A hypothetical question is one that asks your contact to respond to a potential or fictional situation, for example 'How would you feel if ...?' or 'What do you think would happen if ...?' or 'If you were in charge of ... what would you do?'

In answering, your contact feels less threatened by the question and, in effect, tells you what you have to do to win them over. They can respond to your proposition more dispassionately and objectively than they may do otherwise because the situation is hypothetical. They also let you know what they are thinking, and this increases your chances of success. This type of questioning is not manipulative; it's simply a way of ensuring that communication is open and has fewer obstacles than it might have otherwise.

The power of the pause: 'Hmm... go on.'

People generally tend not to like silence during a conversation and will fill the gap if the silence goes on too long. Also, during a conversation we give other visual clues, usually with the eyes, that say what we are thinking. Top connectors combine these two points to encourage the other person to continue talking.

It goes like this: your contact adds something to the conversation by giving you some information. In return you say nothing, but look at him, opening your eyes slightly wider and making the kind of encouraging sounds we make when listening ('Mmm', 'Yes?', 'Uhuh') or inclining your head forward slightly. Your contact is then very likely to elaborate on the information they have just given you.

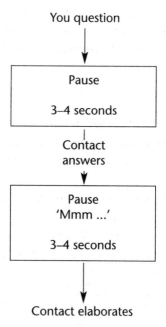

The connector's graveyard

Beware of badly used or inappropriate questions... Welcome to the connector's graveyard.

Closed questions

The number of possible answers to these is small and often predictable, and they often don't yield very much information anyway.

Inappropriately used, they send signals that shout: 'I'm more concerned with what's in my mind, not yours. I'm not really bothered about what you think and feel.' Closed questions are often useful only to gain a quick confirmation of basic facts.

Forced-choice or multiple questions

Like a question in a test with a multiple-choice answer, your contact can only choose the answer closest to how they would like to respond, not what they really want to say. For example, 'Which is your biggest problem at the moment – cash management, your mortgage or the loan repayments?'

The biggest problem at the moment could actually be getting rid of a pushy salesperson.

Leading questions

A poor salesman's ploy, 'leaders' tell the other person what you expect to hear or how you would want them to answer. Often they are more like a statement than a genuine question, for example:

'You don't like it when that happens, do you?'

'It's just like that, isn't it?'

'They always do it this way, don't they?'

Leading questions can be used, with care, when you want to move on to the next point: 'Well, I think we're more or less agreed on that, aren't we?' But make sure that you *are* in agreement before saying it!

Judgemental questions

These simply come across as manipulative and are almost guaranteed to antagonise. Do you recognise these when you have the occasional tiff with a loved one or work colleague? For example: 'How many weeks is it since you tidied your office?' or 'How long are you going to cling to those views?' This question is just a poorly disguised way of saying 'I think you're out of date, mate.'

Questions to gain your contact's commitment

In most instances you can't try to gain your contact's commitment to whatever it is you are offering – yourself, your services or your product – until you have presented your answer to their requirements and they have acknowledged it.

A good way of checking whether you and your contact are ready to agree on the next steps and to draw out any nagging concerns is to ask questions to check if they are happy with your approach. Salespeople call these 'closing' questions, but you can use them in any aspect of connecting. Examples are:

- How do you feel about that?

- How does that strike you?

- Are you happy with everything we have talked about?

- Do you have a date in mind?

- Did you have any other questions about it?

If your contact raises any concerns or objections, it's important for you to get them out into the open and discuss them, otherwise you'll get stalled.

Closing questions

When you are in a position to close, always *ask for what you want*. Be direct and to the point. Don't be coy and hint at it.

There are many types of 'close' and some will be more appropriate for you and your situation than others. Have a look at these:

The direct close

Use this when you are confident of a successful outcome. You have found your contact's needs and requirements, and explained how you can help. You've proved yourself and your contact understands the benefits of what you can offer. If you've handled any objections and worries, and everything seems positive, then ask something like:

'Can we start right away?'

'Are we agreed then? Can we go ahead?'

The step-by-step close

The step-by-step close is ideal when the project you are discussing is large or complicated, or when your contact will have trouble deciding on everything at once.

Break it down into 'chunks' – areas that are easy to agree individually – and discuss them one at a time. Once you have done this, the secret is to recap, covering each area, until it's apparent to both of you that you have covered all the areas you need to agree on. You will then have a 'yes' to the entire project, based on a series of smaller and easier decisions.

The 'if we' close

This is the exception to the rule on timing and if used correctly can soften your approach. The idea is to gain agreement that you can move ahead before even discussing what you will do. At the time when you *clearly* understand your contact's requirements, you say something like: 'I think I can help here. If I can offer you an effective solution to [whatever the problem is], can we go ahead?' The normal response is something like: 'Yes, providing that...'

If nothing else, this approach teases out early concerns and caveats which you can address in your further discussions.

Questions, the ubiquitous tool of the connector

This section has given you an insight into the ways in which you can use questions to empathise with your conversation partner, show interest, control a discussion and, ultimately, help them to decide whether they want you and your services.

I am conscious that the sample questions may appear somewhat 'cold' when set out on a piece of paper. In real conversation you'll be able to add your own warmth, colour and personality to them. Reading sample questions is the equivalent of reading the lyrics on the back of a CD – they look odd and sometimes downright ridiculous without the music to accompany them. Try these questions with the 'music' of your conversation and see how easy it is to blend them into your discussions to guide the outcome. With the right questions you too can become the 'conductor' of the conversation.

So important are questions in many aspects of a connector's role that you'll see other examples throughout the book. They are not intended to repeat what's been said here, rather to complement it by putting questions in the context of the connector's other techniques.

Now let's look at the other side of the coin – listening to the answers you've been given.

Sharpening your Listening Skills

> 'Nature has given to man one tongue, but two ears that we may hear from others twice as much as we speak.'
>
> Epictetus, Greek philosopher

One of the connector's most potent weapons is his ears. They act as antennae to pick up masses of useful information – a contacts' opinions, preferences, sports, business issues, spouse's name, new market opportunities, children and their interests, competitors, political affiliations, short-term vision for the business, wedding anniversary, car, hobbies, IT systems difficulties, and so on.

If these look like a hotch potch of unrelated pieces of information, they are – because that's how the ebb and flow of a conversation goes. And that's why the champion connector needs to constantly have their ears open. Each piece of information is a step towards a stronger relationship.

But listening like a champ takes practice for most of us. It's too easy to mentally 'switch off' and pretend we are listening while going through the motions. We think we can get by without really 'tuning in'. We develop the habitual nod of acknowledgement, the look of concern and the 'front' of understanding. And you can fake it – but not if you really want your listening time to help you to connect.

The ace listener is fully present in the 'here and now', not distracted or daydreaming. They recognise that listening is the way to people's affections. We all want to be heard and to feel that others care about what we have to say. Naturally, then, we warm to those who make us feel special and who treat us as if what we say really matters. Would *you* be more likely to say 'yes' to someone who makes *you* feel important or to someone who seeks to persuade you to see *their* point of view?

Listening is the connector's road to earning a contact's trust and respect. Rapt attention sprinkled with well-placed questions and sincere praise, where due, produces the free-flowing rapport that is the hallmark of all great contact-makers. A super listener who has soaked up the information presented to them like a sponge has real credibility and their comments carry more weight and relevance. Such patience has paid off in the form of vital information that allows them to get to know their contact better. Listening like this can be a stimulating mental activity, not a chore requiring fake nods and smiles.

'I hear what you say!'

- Take five minutes to sit quietly, close your eyes and listen to all the sounds around you. You'll be surprised at how much you can tune into and, consequently, how much you miss normally.

- Be quiet. When someone else is speaking, don't butt in. Discipline yourself to keep quiet rather than rushing in with your own contribution.

- Summarise and paraphrase. Listen to what others are saying, then, to test your understanding, take a few moments to 'play back' the highlights to your conversation companion. It's not as weird as it sounds. The best salespeople use this technique to confirm a customer's needs and issues before suggesting a solution. Ask your conversation partner how well you captured and interpreted the key messages.

TRY THIS

Make tomorrow your listening day. Follow these rules from the moment you get out of bed to the last second before you switch off the light and snuggle under the duvet:

- Allow speakers to complete their points and count at least two seconds of silence before you respond. Don't interrupt.

- Listen in the here and now. Keep up with the speaker. Avoid mentally running on ahead or jumping to conclusions.

- Harness your mental energy to focus on the speaker and understand their message. Bring yourself back from any daydreaming.

- Paraphrase the speaker's remarks where appropriate to practise the technique. Don't just switch the conversation to yourself.

- Assess your performance at the end of the day. What did you do well/poorly and why? Give yourself a mark out of 10 and use your experience as a baseline for other listening encounters in the future.

Effective connectors enter into conversations with a desire to extract useful information or to get to know the other person better, so that they are better able to assist them. They know that they need to listen first if they are to persuade later. They don't request things or plead their case until they have paid attention to others. This means the connector rewards others by listening to them before asking for their co-operation or support.

You already know that the best way to interest people is to appeal to their self-interest. However, you won't know what their interests and desires are until you listen. Great connectors listen receptively because they are hungry for knowledge, enter into conversations expecting to learn and are excited about the opportunity to gain insight. As a result, their genuine interest in learning something new, or just getting to know someone better, turns listening into a mentally stimulating and enjoyable activity. Likewise, your aim should be to get at least one fact or opinion out of every conversation.

Learning and listening are bed-mates. You will find that the more information you capture and retain, the more you will want to listen – and the motivation to learn will feed your desire to listen. You'll soon be picking out key phrases that flag up preferences or roads to a decision. Opinion phrases like 'I like…', 'I can't believe that…', 'My favourite…', 'I really enjoy…' are meat and drink to the good connector. They are clear indicators of the thought patterns of their contact. So too are decision phrases like 'I've decided that…', 'It makes sense to…', 'It's clear that we need to…' You get the picture.

Show you care

But that's not all. To be a champion connector it is not enough to *be* a great listener. You have to *show* your contact that you are listening. You need to give physical and verbal signs that draw attention to your superb listening skills.

There's an obvious reason for this that's often overlooked. When your contact sees how much you care about what they say, they will look more favourably on you. And when it's your turn to speak, they will return the courtesy and listen better. They will trust you and confide in you (would you confide in someone who doesn't listen to you?) and there is no better way to make connections with people and gain their respect than to show others that you really hear what they say.

Here's how the pros do it:

1. Get in line

They align themselves physically with the speaker, not copying every movement, but mirroring their general position. Here's a great tip from the social anthropologists: carry your head, shoulders and legs in a similar way and in particular try to align your shoulders with those of the speaker. Try it with shoulders in, and out, of alignment and notice the difference in rapport. It's fascinating.

2. Acknowledge with occasional 'listening sounds' such as 'hmm' and 'uh-huh'

People need to *hear* that you are listening and be encouraged to go on. Verbal cues, including 'Yes', 'Go on', 'I see' and 'Tell me more', do exactly that ... if used in moderation. Like everything, don't overdo it, otherwise it sounds false and distracting. If you are listening carefully your verbal 'cue' points should come naturally anyway.

3. Look, really look

An obvious one, but so easily ignored. We've all seen the stereotypical breakfast scene where the wife is talking and her husband is grunting meaninglessly behind his newspaper. The simple rule is to concentrate on the speaker, look them in the face and not have your eyes darting all over the place. Even if you are listening, 'wandering eyes' will give your contact the feeling that there is something far more interesting going on somewhere else – and your relationship will take a couple of steps backwards as a result.

4. Move closer

Without intruding on your contact's personal space, move closer or lean forward to give the physical cue that you are interested and want to make sure you hear every word they say.

5. Get your body involved

We picked up on the verbal cues earlier. Here we are talking about non-spoken ways of encouraging your contact to speak and, at the same time, demonstrate that you are listening intently. These non-verbal clues range from nodding your head, smiling and animated facial expressions (appropriate to the nature of the conversation, of course) to genuine laughter. The key, again, is not to overdo it, and to use variety in your expressions. Watch how other people respond to you when you are speaking. Can you adopt any of their best non-verbal cues and build them into your own repertoire?

6. The power of playback

A small difference in understanding at the start of a conversation may be imperceptible but as the conversation progresses it may grow into a major divide. If you check your understanding of the other person's point of view, concerns, intended actions or whatever, you avoid the danger of an ever-widening gulf. It shows you have been listening, are interested in their opinions and are concerned about getting things right.

Regularly paraphrase your understanding of what the other person has said. Such 'playback' is a good way of punctuating the discussion part-way through a conversation. At the end of a conversation it's a nice way to round off with a final check of your understanding.

Listening to remember

One of the real benefits of listening is retaining key facts about others and delighting them by showing that you remember. We love it when someone recalls exactly what we said or remembers an occasion that is special to us such as a birthday or anniversary. Clearly, not all of your contacts would feel it appropriate to receive a formal birthday card, and less so an anniversary card, but almost all of us would welcome a quick call or email to say 'Congratulations' when it is appropriate and, what's more, we'll feel closer to the person who has taken the time to remember.

What does this have to do with building your network of connections? Well, when you recall someone's birthday or some other (non-embarrassing, non privacy-threatening) item – you demonstrate that they count in your eyes. Indeed, it is hard to resist the allure of someone who successfully steps into our world and understands what makes us tick.

The knack, of course, is to make mental notes of what others say as part of your listening process. You'll be amazed at what you'll pick up – the names of spouses, children and wider family members, your contact's interests, hobbies, holiday plans, car... More important than your own amazement at what information you can glean from conversation is the impression you will make on your contact. Often they will be deeply moved by your ability to recall – and act on – what they said, possibly months after they had uttered the 'gem' of information.

In this way you will reap all kinds of reward. You will earn trust and gain respect, and develop the inside track on how that person thinks. With listening skills in such short supply, you will stand out even more. Many (poor) networkers don't even try to retain the basic details of their contacts. They are too concerned with their own agenda and, as a result, squander countless opportunities to make people feel special. For them, networking appears to offer little return, and by their actions they are proved right. We'll be looking at how to remember names and faces later, but in the meantime...

TRY THIS

A superb connector is one who listens effectively. They'll want to know:

- What the other person thinks and feels.

- What they need and want.

- Their most important desire right now.

- What problems, real or potential, stand between them and the achievement of their goals.

However, to listen for long periods with the same level of intensity is actually impossible. So you need to practise 'in–out' listening.

This means that you listen intently until you hear something that demands a response from you. That response may be to make a note of what they said, make a comment or even simply nod your head to demonstrate that you have heard and understand. The small action will be enough to give your brain a break and give you the chance to tune in again. Your brain processes information and remembers by making connections. By actively making connections with what you hear, you will remember better and be able to listen effectively for longer.

CHAPTER 5

How to Work a Room

BUSINESS GATHERINGS LIKE cocktail parties, receptions, conferences, association meetings and seminars all have a social element to them. These are the arenas where the connector's skills of listening, questioning, being interested and building rapport come to the fore. These functions are a meeting-place where, if you know how to do it, you'll make new contacts that may lead to new friendships or new business. You'll also have interesting conversations and widen the circle of people you know.

The true connectors know how to 'work a room'. If you could be a fly on the wall at a cocktail party, for example, you'd see them circulating easily and with grace around the room, meeting, greeting and talking to people in a way that looks and sounds sincere. It's evident that they know how to start, develop and end lively and interesting conversations that build rapport – and maybe generate new work opportunities for themselves or others. Wouldn't you like to be like that? You can be, if you emulate the techniques they use.

You'll already have many of these skills under your belt. We've all had some experience of introducing ourselves, making conversation with people we've not met before, saying our goodbyes and moving on. Just reading this paragraph may, however, have got the hairs standing up on the back of your neck. Not everyone likes this sort of networking environment. In fact, in a study of social fears undertaken in the United States in 1998, people rated 'meeting new people in an unfamiliar environment' as a close second to unrehearsed public speaking!

Perhaps it's because we feel we need to 'perform' and be at our most witty and charming, that we can feel nervous, tense and downright irritable before we go to an event. Some of us even feel physically sick beforehand. The psychologists have a term for it (don't they always?): 'social phobia'.

The reality is that, depending on the occasion, most of us have some anxiety about going into unfamiliar social situations. Yes, it is uncomfortable walking into a room full of people you don't know – and it's even worse when you need to make a good impression. For some reason (your comfort zone, actually) all of your personality and social skills seem to drain away when you feel out of your depth.

But when you do know how to work a room you'll feel better about yourself, make great social and business contacts and, most important of all, you'll be able to make others feel more comfortable too. Your confidence will attract them to you and make them want to know you better.

If you are a regular function-goer you've probably looked around on occasions when your conversation is not going well and sensed that everyone else in the room is completely at ease – but it's not true. In experiments in these circumstances researchers found that while most people were feeling 'uncertain', to others they appeared relaxed. So don't believe that it's only you who feels apprehensive on these occasions – almost everyone there is likely to feel exactly the same as you! The exceptions, of course, are the connectors who, nervous or not, know exactly what to do.

The Social Rules of Working a Room

Let's get a handle on the social rules of networking situations like these. When you are in a 'business social' situation, the normal social rules you work to in everyday life change somewhat. Here are the key areas of difference:

- **People expect to be approached by 'strangers'** If you were walking down the street and a stranger approached you, you'd most likely take a step back and be on your guard. The rules are reversed in business function situations, however. There, it is polite and accepted practice to move around the room introducing yourself. As a result people expect to be approached by people they don't know and, nine times out of ten, will positively welcome it.

- **People want to move around** In my experience a lot of people new to networking have difficulty with this. They feel that once they've latched onto a conversation partner or two it is impolite to move on, and their networking efforts end right there. In reality, at functions where people are there to meet others and interact, they want to move around and make new contacts. This fact leads nicely to the next social protocol.

- **Conversations can be short** If you want to work a room effectively it means your conversations have to be short – but short doesn't necessarily mean 'superficial'. It's quite possible to have a thought-provoking, stimulating ten-minute conversation with a new contact that builds all the rapport you need. Where appropriate, you can gain their permission to stay in touch (more later) so that you can explore the areas you discussed in more detail another time.

Social scientists put the average conversation in a networking situation at around 15 minutes. Experienced event-goers will recognise that this equates to six potentially new contacts at an average drinks reception. That's good going, if you know how to hold conversations with contacts you wish to build rapport with.

■ **Overselling is a sin** Picture the scene. Jack, the double-glazing salesman you've just met, has you pinned in a corner of the room. The cocktail-party guests drift past and there's a hum of polite social chit-chat. But not for you and Jack. He's determined to use this networking function to make a sale. 'After all, that's what all this networking is about,' he says. His hard-sell tactics lead you to a feeling that you won't get out of the place alive unless you give in to his verbal assault and say 'yes'.

Sounds a ridiculous scenario, doesn't it? But it's not quite so far-fetched, as it's happened to me! I use the story to illustrate the point that nobody wants to be sold to at a networking function. It's not good social or business practice, and your chances of success aren't good anyway.

Business socials are for rapport-building and identifying areas of mutual interest. It's a time for Jack the double-glazing salesman to find out a little about me, to ask about my interests, my family, my home – anything except whether I want double glazing. If I think he seems like a nice chap and gains my trust, I'll probably reciprocate and ask what he does for a living. Maybe then we'll get to talking about his business. If I am in the market for double glazing and what he tells me leads me to think that it's worth considering what I should do with my windows, then he's done his job. People buy from people they trust, and trust has to be earned.

How to Meet the People You Want to Meet

Working a room isn't about buzzing around the premises introducing yourself and having fleeting half-conversations with fellow guests. Sure, that's one way to meet a lot of folk, but it's unlikely that you'll have given yourself sufficient time to make an impact.

That's not to decry this approach, however. I'd much rather someone did this (and it takes courage to do it) than sit in the corner talking to no one, or stay with the same conversation partner until you've exhausted all topics.

Nevertheless, there is a better way – the way the real 'room workers' operate. In the business context, much of it depends on research. Focusing in advance on who is likely to be most relevant to you is a superb strategy for concentrating your efforts on meeting a few people rather than trying to 'press the flesh' with everyone in the room in the style of a politician in the race for the White House.

At purely social functions, the scenario changes a little. You could ask the host in advance for a rundown of who's coming and a copy of the invitee list, but you'll appear somewhat cold and mercenary in the process. Not a good start. The way the pros do it at social gatherings is by asking non-threatening and 'soft' questions of the host when they get there.

Get a 'feel' for your fellow guests

Let's look at social functions first, then ease our way into more business-oriented events like seminars and other business functions. Now get into character (and your party clothes) and visualise this. You have been invited to drinks at a business associate's house. You anticipate knowing no one there. How do you suss out who's who and identify those people who are most likely to see your value to them?

Talking to *anyone* is great fun if you ask the right questions and are genuinely interested in them. But you bought this book in order to learn the secrets of the champion networkers, so here goes.

You arrive at the home of your contact and the drinks reception is in full swing. When you've said 'Hello' to the host and entered into some social chit-chat, say, 'You've got a full house here. Are many people local?' Most hosts will then identify any neighbours that have been invited. You could then follow on naturally with other questions about the group, for example: 'Is there anyone else from [my sector/profession] here?' Your host will usually be able to tell you who is in your line of business and often will give you an idea what the other guests do with their time too.

If not, simply say: 'I don't know anyone here tonight. Would you mind giving me a quick rundown of a few of the people to help me to settle in?' This is an unusual question, but sometimes it needs to be asked. You've stated your reason why you've asked it – you want to settle in quickly – and your host will understand your position. They'll normally do one of two things, depending on how well they know you and the time they have. Either they'll give you a quick rundown of guests, which usually includes their profession and place of origin, or they'll offer to introduce you to someone. The rundown of guests is great for a connector because this is the closest thing they will get to a written guest list in the business context.

Ask two opening questions

When talking to guests, top connectors have two questions in their armoury that they use when the right conditions arise.

The first question is: 'How do you know the host?' This question usually elicits information about the relationship between host and guest and, if it's a business one, they usually say what area of business they are in. If not, it's an easy follow-up question to ask: 'And what line of business are you in?'

The second question is: 'Do you know many people here?' If the person knows a few, they will usually provide a little 'potted history' of who's who and their relationship with them.

Not only are these safe conversation topics (your fellow guest can reveal as much or as little as they prefer), but they also provide the signposts for the connector on where to go next. The answers give them some background information to guide the conversation and show how best they might be able to add value to their future conversation partner.

Get to know that special person

Now, how to meet that person who you would like to get to know better? A sophisticated conversation partner, on hearing you say that you are in a similar field to another guest, may say, 'I'll introduce you later.' Sounds too good to be true, and it usually is.

Instead, depending on the rapport you have created with your conversation partner, you could say: 'As we're in the same field, I'd be very interested in meeting [fellow guest]. I wonder, would you mind introducing me later?' Most fellow guests will offer to do so when you've finished your conversation. But sometimes, for whatever reason, it doesn't happen (your intended contact has moved elsewhere in the room or is engrossed in conversation, or your existing conversation partner has simply forgotten or is reticent about doing it). Don't despair, it doesn't make much difference anyway.

All you do now is approach your contact and say, 'Hello, I'm ... I hope you don't mind me introducing myself but I was talking with [previous person] earlier, who was telling me that you are in the [sector/profession]. I work with XYZ Corporation ...' and then explain the relevance. Ask questions about their situation; don't launch into your life history.

There are other techniques for getting into a conversation which can provide a springboard for other connections. You could be bold and say, for example, 'I hope you don't mind, I don't know anyone here but you looked friendly so I thought I'd introduce myself. I'm ... from XYZ Corporation. May I join you?'

Ease your way into groups

You can even use the following classic approach to ease your way into a group of people if you feel confident about yourself. Simply say: 'You look as if you are [having fun/enjoying yourselves/having an interesting discussion], would you mind if I joined you?' The vast majority of the people will open up and welcome you because you've explained your rationale for joining them and flattered them in the process.

A tip, though: listen to what the group is talking about before you attempt to enter it. For all you know it may be something very private and your perfectly executed approach could be rebuffed for that reason alone.

If the conversation is a general one and you feel it's OK to join in, make sure that you address your opening remarks to the person who is speaking. This is not only social protocol, it's sound business sense. Social psychologists have proved that if you address your first comments to anyone other than the speaker, you alienate the speaker because you've taken their audience away from them. So, speak to the speaker first, engage in the group discussion in the normal way and find a good time later to introduce yourself if people in the group don't already know you.

If the discussion topic is something you can contribute to from your own knowledge, great. If not, you can still join, but be prepared to listen and ask intelligent questions based on the discussion. It's a harder road, but you'll learn something and will have demonstrated that you are interested in the people in the group and their perspective on the subject.

If you are a member of the host team at a business function it's much easier to break into a group, because you have a right to do so. Checking that everyone has had something to eat and drink and asking any other 'Are you all right?' type of questions allows you to join the group.

However, the very best way to join a group is to be invited in by others. A good starting-point is making eye contact with someone you know already. Often this alone will signal to them that you would like to join in.

TRY THIS

Make a conscious decision to approach people whom you might not normally speak to. Armed with your repertoire of introductory conversation openers, you should have no difficulty in making a good first impression and developing some rapport. If you are rejected for whatever reason, use the 'So what?' approach. They didn't have the pleasure of knowing you in the first place and have missed the golden opportunity to get to know you now. It's their loss.

In all seriousness, the more people you meet, the less fazed you will be by the process. And you will recognise that you will 'win' far more than you lose in the developing connections game.

Turning a Social Chat into a Business Conversation

Conversation in a business setting – a cocktail party or the refreshments session before or after a seminar or conference, for example – can be compared to driving a car in that you need the right gear at the right time. First gear is the start of the conversation, the small talk area; second gear is achieved by changing from social pleasantries into a more business-focused discussion. Third is exploring specific aspects of the business conversation that are of interest to both parties, and fourth gear is the zone where things have gone well and you are seeking your conversation partner's permission to stay in touch.

The changing gears analogy is a good one because, as any driver will tell you, trying to start off in third gear, for example, usually requires much greater effort than first and, indeed, the car (just like your conversation) is in danger of stalling. Why? Because you've entered at the wrong point, skipped a couple of gears, and such a conversation often gets off to a juddering start.

Just as an advanced driver moves effortlessly through the gears, so too the experienced connector. The advanced driver also knows when it is possible to jump gears, as does the connector. But for the purposes of this book let's assume that you work through the conversation gears in a logical order with people you've not met before.

The emphasis in this section is placed on conversation in a business setting, as most people have difficulty in the following areas:

- Starting a conversation with someone they don't know.

- Turning a social 'chat' into a business discussion.

- Gaining their conversation partner's permission to stay in touch.

- Following up in an elegant and effective way.

Some connectors may take as little as five minutes to go through the gears, while in other conversations the stages may take an hour or more. Some chats, of course, will draw to a halt at any point between first and fourth gear. There may be a number of reasons for this, but you'll know by now that the factors that are critical to moving it along are:

- Using your self-introduction to interest your conversation partner in you and what you have to say.

- Building rapport in the very early stages of the discussion and continuing it.

- Using non-threatening questions to help guide the direction of the chat.

- Listening actively so that you really hear what is being said and can assess the implication of the messages.

Conversation is not a mechanical process and it can meander about all over the place in real life. Nevertheless, the various stages of this model do help you to get a feel for where you are in the discussion at any point in time.

Now you know the theory, let's move on to some of the specific actions attached to each stage. Every person is different and every situation will require a tailored approach, but nevertheless you need a number of standard options at your disposal.

'What's happening?'

The first thing to do is to be prepared for conversation by keeping yourself up to speed with the latest big news.

Keeping up with the news doesn't mean digesting the *Financial Times* line by line, but it does mean picking up the major news stories of the day. What's happening in business, sport, the economy and politics right now? Even the weather forecast is valuable! Most people can get what they need for this from a ten-minute scan of the daily newspaper or by picking up the TV and radio news broadcasts.

If you don't know what's going on, you'll be at a disadvantage in comparison to those who obviously do – no one would have wanted to be the last person in the room to know that John F. Kennedy had been shot, for example. That would have certainly given the (correct) impression that you didn't have your finger on the pulse. In a ridiculous way, the same feeling of 'not in touch' can be engendered in the mind of a sports fanatic contact if you don't know the result of last night's big game.

The message is: do your homework and be interested in what's going on. It won't take long and it will pay great dividends in making it easier for you to both start and join in with 'social' conversations.

Prepare your views

Now that you've heard the latest news, think about it. What are the implications of what's happening? Thinking through your views in this way will help you to articulate your opinions far better than if you had to give them 'off the cuff'.

What will the attendees be thinking about?

Most business functions are called with a specific purpose in mind – perhaps to provide information, to inform of changes, to promote something, to celebrate success or to mark an occasion. Whatever the reason, give some consideration to what the attendees are likely to be thinking about.

For example, if you're attending a business awards function the attendees will be wondering who's won the various categories. The top connector will consider where the 'collective mind' is and form their own opinion in advance. Who should win? Why? Who won last year? The connector will then have the confidence to discuss the awards with anyone they meet in their networking, and will sound both knowledgeable and interesting.

Opening lines

Opening lines are like placing the car's gear stick into first. There's no need for fancy moves at this stage. That's why the selection of openers below will seem banal. They do nothing more than get you started on the conversation road.

The fail-safe line, mentioned already, is 'Hello, can I introduce myself? I'm …' It's a very rare occasion indeed when a potential conversation partner says 'no'!

You've got the conversation going, so what's next? Much depends on the circumstances, but you could employ permutations of 'neutral' questions like those below. Bear in mind that it's a conversation, not an interrogation, so you'll need to play your part in giving information back to the other person.

If the words don't sound right to you on these pages that's partly because small talk doesn't easily transfer onto paper. Just get a feel for the type of questions to ask and use whatever words and phrases you feel comfortable with. How about these first-gear questions to get your conversation off to a smooth start:

- Have you come far?
- How was the traffic?
- Did you manage to get a parking spot all right?
- Have you been here/to this event before?
- Do you know many people here?
- Have you had anything to eat/drink yet?

Nothing sparkling about any of these, but remember, the aim is to just get the conversation going.

It's important in the early stages to share some information about yourself. The best exponents of this technique give information then tag a question on the end so that they get something back. For example, when talking about getting to the venue, you might say: 'It seems as though the traffic is getting worse just lately. It takes me an extra ten minutes to get to the office on East Street from my home in Anytown. *Is it the same for you?'*

The answer can open up the opportunity for the connector to ask further questions like:

- In which area do you live?

- Where is your office?

- What route do you take?

- Do you do a lot of driving in your job?

A statement with a question 'tag' is the elegant way for a connector to seek information. Here's another one designed to get a feeling for a conversation partner's leisure interests. At an appropriate point in the conversation (only you will know when) you say: 'It's been a hectic week for me this week. I'm certainly looking forward to my weekend game of golf. It's my way to unwind... *Do you play at all?'*

If they do, then your conversation is up and running. If they don't, you may say one of the following:

- What do *you* do with your leisure time?

- Do you play any sports?

- Have you anything special planned for the weekend?

The question you ask will depend on the person you are speaking to, but you can imagine that the answers you get to those questions will range from yes, they are interested in some sport or other, to no, they are not. If they are, you'll explore that, if not, you'll leave the subject well alone. Normally people will tell you what they are interested in without you having to prise it out of them.

TRY THIS

Write down the five conversation starters that you would feel most comfortable with. Pick them from this book or make them up yourself. The idea is to make sure you have a small repertoire at the front of your mind so that you are not stuck for words when you need them to ease yourself into a conversation.

Take a few seconds after every event to review whether your conversation starter worked. If it did, keep it in your repertoire; if it didn't, ask yourself why. If it doesn't get the desired response after trying it on a few occasions, ditch it for a better one. Don't flog a dead horse.

Moving smoothly on to business

At many business functions where people wear name badges it's easy to get onto a business footing by introducing yourself, looking at the person's badge and saying: 'What does XYZ Corporation do?' If you already know the company, you would probably say: 'I see you're with XYZ Corporation... What's your role there?'

If people don't wear badges at the function, as long as you've 'teed up' the social discussion earlier, it's an easy follow on to ask 'And what area of business are you in?'

So far so obvious, but how do you really get under the skin of what a person and their business are up to? There are three questions that will solve your problem.

'Are you busy at the moment?' is the gentlest, but often the most effective business conversation opener going. You can see that you can easily slot this question in behind your social opener. Indeed, on the right occasion, you can ask it very quickly after you've made your introductions. Its power comes from the fact that however the question is answered there is a natural follow on:

'Are you busy at the moment?'
'No, not really.'
'Oh, why's that...?'

'Are you busy at the moment?'
'Yes, very.'
'Oh, why's that...?

The answer is like a fork in the road, with both paths leading you to a conversation which explores a person's present situation in the context of their business. Such discussions are normally great for building empathy through careful listening and questioning, and can provide information on areas where you may be able to help.

There are two other alternatives. Not rocket science, but incredibly effective. 'How's business?' is broad enough to be non-threatening to most people, but an even better question is 'What do you see on the horizon for your business over the next few months?' Often connectors will 'soften' this question by giving a preamble statement beforehand, something like: 'I see that the Government is still worried about a recession, but our business still appears to be holding up well... What do you see on the horizon for your business/sector over the next few months?'

Occasionally people are not happy to share what's going on in their business with a relative stranger. That's when connectors 'distance' themselves by asking what's happening in the sector instead of their conversation partner's business. In this case they will be happy to share what's going on in their industry generally.

Either way, should they choose to answer the question from their sector or own business perspective, in effect they are telling you the big issues of the moment and while they may be talking about their sector generally, it's very likely that their comments are steeped in what's going on in their own business situation.

Track back

Often in a wide-ranging conversation, the talk may move between social and business chat, or take a route that leads away from an area of particular interest to the connector. This is where they score with active listening and incisive questioning. Luckily, it's not difficult.

What connectors do is to remember what their conversation partner said earlier about the topic the connector is interested in and when there's an appropriate break in the conversation, say:

'I was interested in your comment earlier about... *How do you see...?*

or

'You mentioned earlier that... *I'd be interested in how you...?'*

Normally your conversation partner will be flattered that you have been paying close attention to what they have to say and will repay you with more information on the area in question.

Converse in context

Gaining an understanding of why people go to business events can often provide a pathway to new opportunities. Asking people what attracted them to the event and, if it's an information-sharing type of event like a seminar, how the topics covered impact on them and their business is a great way to get a feel for the issues they are facing and the opportunities available to them.

TRY THIS

Move gently from social to business conversation and avoid any sense of 'selling' by making statements and asking questions. In this way you can identify areas where you or others may be able to help the person you are speaking to.

Circulating with Elegance and Effect

One of the major difficulties expressed by delegates on my working the room training courses is how to finish a conversation and move on to talk with others. Part of the secret is gaining permission to stay in touch (if you want to) and the best way to signal that the chat is drawing to a natural close is to ask for a card. In so doing you can restate what you have agreed to do.

But what do you do then? You can make moving on as painless as possible by:

- Introducing the person to someone else you know – a colleague, work associate, friend or anyone else you feel comfortable approaching to introduce your new-found conversation partner.

- Being brave enough to be upfront about moving on by saying something like 'It's been very nice talking to you, perhaps we can catch up later.' It's the 'perhaps we can catch up later' that softens the leaving line. It says in a few words that you've enjoyed your chat and would like to talk some more another time, and gives them the affirmation that they are liked.

IN PRACTICE

One management consultant I came across used the line 'I've really enjoyed our conversation. Thank you. I did promise I'd meet a couple of clients here today, so I'd better track them down. So, if you'll excuse me … Perhaps we can catch up later.'

Whether he really had clients he'd arranged to meet is almost academic. His rationale was that the approach demonstrated professionalism and empathy at the same time – professionalism in the sense that he had promised something and needed to deliver on it, and empathy by telling his conversation partner that he had enjoyed their chat and expressed an interest in getting back together later.

The chances of them meeting up again were slim, of course, unless he had agreed a specific follow-up action and identified ways in which he or others could help.

If you want to gain permission to stay in touch, ask for a card and close the conversation by agreeing a follow-up action. Add your elegant leaving line and move on. After you've had experience doing this a number of times it will become second nature.

Learn from the Champion 'Room Workers'

Top connectors have other techniques for making sure they get the best chance to meet the people they want to meet. Put together, these tricks of the trade give them the edge.

The sophisticated room worker's technique is to face the door so that they can see their clients, friends and potential new contacts – even people they want to avoid – entering the room without taking their focus off the person they are talking to. Nothing is calculated to destroy rapport more quickly than gazing around the room when you should have your attention on your conversation partner.

Another trick is to join contacts in the line for food and drink, because making small talk is easy there. It's easy to start a conversation by commenting on anything to do with the situation.

Just one word of advice before we get into some more examples of opening remarks – make sure your comments are positive ones. If not, you're in danger of your new conversation partner marking you down as a moaning Minnie. Why? Because their 'sample' of your tone and attitude is one of negativity. Even if your comments are valid, it's best to save them for later in the conversation when the other person has a more positive picture of your attitude.

At the buffet, depending on your conversational style, you could say anything from 'There's certainly plenty of choice here' or 'They've obviously worked hard on the buffet' to 'I think my diet may be going out of the window tonight.' These are innocuous comments with a complimentary twist, designed to elicit a comment from your fellow muncher, an ice-breaker from which you can move to introduce yourself or discuss other aspects of the event.

At the bar, for example, depending on the circumstances, you could say: 'They look busy/quiet tonight' or 'I've not stopped all day and I'm ready for a cold drink now' or 'Why don't you go before me, mine's quite a large order' (if it is!). Your contact will be appreciative of your gesture and will open up easily.

Again, these are just gentle 'connecting' comments that may or may not lead to more in-depth discussions; your own instinct will tell you which. However, even if the conversation is very short, the connector has done their job in engaging their contact and made themselves known. It will be much easier later to start a conversation because they now know each other, however slightly.

Keep close, at the right time

At pre-event refreshments like seminars or conferences, the best connectors know that timing is the key to making the most of the person they sit next to. Just this move alone could make the difference between landing your next piece of work or the assignment going to your competitor.

Engineering whom you sit next to requires good planning and being a bit streetwise. For example, a connector is at a seminar to learn the latest developments in outsourcing and, having already reviewed the guest list, has the goal of meeting three prospective clients. In particular the connector would like to meet Karen Fenwick, the marketing director of Academy plc.

The connector knows what Karen looks like, having already asked the receptionist to say when she has arrived. But, rather than immediately walk over to her, he checks the time – ten minutes to go until the start of the seminar. Too soon. The connector waits for another five minutes, then makes the move to get into polite conversation with Karen about her business and issues in the sector/profession (having read up about them, of course, in researching the three contacts).

Karen is impressed by the connector's knowledge by the time the delegates are called to take their seats in the seminar room. 'I've enjoyed our conversation,' the connector says. 'Would you mind if I joined you in the seminar?' Unless there's a specific reason why not (and there could be) her answer will be: 'No, of course not.' And the connector takes the opportunity to make a few pertinent comments to demonstrate their knowledge and build a bond for the duration of the event.

Now that's the difference between a run-of-the-mill networker and a real connector.

Stand at the crossroads

Where would you stand if you wanted to meet most people at a business function – in the corner of the room or the middle? Actually, it's a trick question, because neither answer is right.

Psychologists who have studied this arena of social interaction have, however, provided some great clues for us to use. Think again about what people do when they attend such gatherings. They get a drink from the bar, if there's buffet-style food they'll visit that table too, and they'll invariably need to pay a visit to the boys' or girls' room sometime during the event. When you know the locations of these 'honey pots' you'll know the invisible thoroughfare that people will use.

One connector friend of mine, when not seeking to make contact with anyone specific, would station himself midway between the buffet and the toilets, as he figured that most folk would come past sooner or later!

TRY THIS

Next time you are at a function, observe the flows of people and see if there is an invisible highway. Be aware that where you position yourself in the room could have a lot to do with how many opportunities you have to meet people.

Apply some common sense to this principle, though. If you find that the crossroads of the invisible thoroughfare between the bar and the food is the middle of the dance floor, you won't do your credibility as a networker much good if you stand there alone, drink in hand!

Being a Great Host

No matter whether you are holding a party at your own home or are hosting a function on behalf of your organisation, you'll want the event to go well and, on a personal level, to be thought of as an excellent host.

While most of the tips on being a good host are obvious, there are a few moves that help connectors make their events enjoyable and productive. The starting-point is to make people feel comfortable. The reason is that the vast majority of people don't feel comfortable in social or business-social situations. And if they are uncomfortable they shrink back into their 'shell', interact less and generally don't have a good time. The host's primary objective, then, is to make people feel welcome and 'at home'. Here are some ways to do it:

Move forward to meet and greet

Psychologists have done a lot of work in this area and concluded that if you move forward to meet and greet people, their impression of you will be far more favourable than if you wait for them to enter your personal space to greet you. So, if you want people to think more of you even before you've opened your mouth, just move forward with open gestures and say 'Hello.' Handshakes and hugs depend on the situation you find yourself in, but this meeting and greeting stage lays the foundation for making contacts feel welcome and special.

Break the ice with food and drink

As a host you have the ideal opportunity to speak to anyone at your function by asking if they have enough food and drink. In most situations it's appropriate for the host to check if the arrangements are to their guests' liking. I've seen great connectors do nothing more all evening than to approach individuals and groups of people and ask questions ranging from 'Have you had anything to drink yet?' and 'Just to let you know, the food is available now' to 'Just checking that you've had something to eat... Yes, was it all right?' You get the picture.

By asking such questions, not only are you being a courteous and good host in looking after your guests' interests, but you are also mingling with a purpose and showing that you are in control of the situation. What's more, once you've broken the ice with someone by asking a question like those above, it's easy to continue the conversation in any direction you like.

'Meet my important friend ...'

Great connectors have developed the skill of introducing others. We've already talked about creating your own 30-second preview which positions you as an open and interesting person to talk to, now let's look at how to help others through your introductions.

The way the best room workers do it is to introduce people as if they are *really* important to them, providing additional explanatory information with a compliment woven in. Here are a few examples so that you get the idea:

'Jane, I'd like you to meet Jack. Jack and I go way back to school days. We used to sit together at the back of the class planning our next bit of fun.'

'Joe, can I introduce Janice? Janice has just advised us on one of our biggest property transactions.'

'Eric, this is Marie, our next-door neighbour and very good friend.'

Connectors do their best to make introductions in this way. Where appropriate, they'll also provide some detail on the other person too. Taking the example above as a model:

'Eric, this is Marie, our next-door neighbour and very good friend.'

Then to Marie: 'Eric's a doctor at GMP Hospital. He specialises in the study of children's medicine.'

In this example, the connector host has taken the time (literally a few seconds) to give a potted history of both people, flattered them at the same time and provided plenty of 'hooks' for them to start a lively and interesting conversation. Contrast that with the usual 'Jane, this is Eric' type of introduction.

At first extending your introductions in this way may feel awkward, but once you get into the swing of it you'll find that you do it without thinking.

TRY THIS

At your next networking event put yourself mentally in the position of 'host' even if you are not hosting. You'll behave differently and probably feel that you have far more confidence in approaching people and generally looking after their interests. There is a strong message here for how to make the most of events by using a 'host' mentality. Give it a go. You'll be surprised at the results.

Help your guests feel at home

It's worth emphasising again that the host's major role is to make guests feel comfortable. They do that by making sure that they are fed and watered properly and are in a position to enjoy convivial conversation (that's where good introductions come in), and they make sure they are seen to be looking after their guests, so that they feel reassured.

It's only when people feel comfortable that they begin to open up and share their views, insights and information. Trying to force a relationship before the comfort stage is counter-productive, as all those salespeople who have attempted to sell timeshare homes will know.

IN PRACTICE

> People remember the interest, warmth and enthusiasm they feel from you, not the words. The best opening line is a smile and 'Hello, I'm ...'

Hosting for an Organisation

At the corporate level, if you are a member of the host organisation's team, make sure you all get together beforehand for a pre-event briefing. The purpose is to discuss who is coming to your event, whether anyone knows specific contacts already and to identify which of your colleagues would also like to meet them. It's then a simple task to agree to make an introduction at an appropriate time during the function.

So far, so basic. However, you would be amazed how many organisations I've trained that don't hold pre-event briefings. As a result, the host team has no idea who they would each like to meet or who should be responsible for looking after whom. In practice this means that some contacts get smothered with attention from several hosts while others are hardly spoken to, or even acknowledged!

IN PRACTICE

> A classic example of where a team of hosts needs to work together to maximise the effectiveness of their contact-making is in the Big 5 accountancy firms. One far-sighted firm a few years back recognised that its hosts (specialists from the various areas of the business like audit, tax, corporate finance and management consultancy) were gaining few new opportunities from its highly acclaimed but costly tax and accountancy update seminars. These

events usually attracted well over 200 delegates but seemed to bring in very little new business.

To find out why, the organisers put a video camera high up in the corner of the room at the next event to observe the proceedings. When the film was analysed, the conclusions were dynamite! It became patently clear why the hosts were not getting the business they expected from the event.

Because the hosts didn't have a briefing session before the event, no one had any responsibility for looking after specific guests. This meant that the hosts simply 'did their own thing' on the day. The outcome was that some clients were spoken to by several hosts, while others hardly got a word from anyone. And, the worst sin, some prospective clients were never spoken to at all!

The reason was easy to fathom and had a lot to do with the firm's organisation of the event and with individuals' 'comfort zones'. As there was no agreed plan of who should talk to whom, hosts tended to talk either to their colleagues or to the clients with whom they felt most comfortable. Left out in the cold were other clients and the group of people they needed to impress most – their prospective clients – many of whom were not known personally by the hosts.

On playing back the video footage the senior partners of the firm were horrified to see that key decision-makers at some of their 'top target' organisations were not spoken to at all by the hosts, apart from the receptionist giving out the name badges. One can only guess at the impression left in the minds of those prospective clients, but 'friendly', 'caring' and 'professional' don't feature highly.

No wonder very few new business opportunities were generated at the function. The hosts were not even getting to first base by speaking to all guests. They failed the common courtesy test – but resolved to put it right. Over the next year they implemented changes that transformed the pay-back from their events.

Here's how they did it…

Plan the action, action the plan

The firm now holds hosts' briefings before every event, going through the guest list, identifying who knows whom and allocating responsibility for making contact with them. As a consequence everyone knows exactly what they have to do and the need to introduce contacts to others has created a great deal more interaction at their events. Previously there was a subdued 'hum' of conversation at such functions. Now there is an energy about the place as people move around, are introduced to new contacts and start building new relationships.

Work as a team, and have your target contacts brought to you

By knowing, as a team, which specialist colleague wished to be introduced to a contact of another, the whole effort of networking became easier. Instead of a group of hosts working as individuals and scouring the room looking at name badges in the hope of locating the next contact on their 'target' list, they could literally have their contact brought to them.

It worked like this: when a host was talking to a target contact of another colleague, at an appropriate point in the conversation they would say: 'When we were talking about this event my colleague [John Smith] expressed an interest in meeting you today. Perhaps I can introduce you to him. He's a specialist in...'

Feedback on this approach was immensely positive. The vast majority of delegates were pleased that someone had expressed a deep interest in meeting them and were happy to be introduced. It helped them to network. The added advantage to the host was that once they had introduced their guest to John Smith, after a suitable period of time they could make their excuses ('I see a client of mine over there and must have a quick word'), leave the conversation and get on with the job of connecting with others.

A good reception desk can transform your business

To meet the people you want to meet easily and professionally, ask the reception desk at your function to let you know when your target contact has arrived (it even works at other people's events too!) In practice this means that you will either arrange for the receptionist to bring the newly arrived guest directly to you, or ask them to inform you when your contact has arrived.

Unusual? Yes, but if it is done with decorum, the process works like a charm. You go to the person manning the reception desk and say: 'There are three people I'd really like to meet today. [Mark them discreetly on the receptionist's checklist.] When they arrive, would you bring them over to me by saying: "Mr Timperley really wanted to meet you today and asked if I would let him know when you arrived, Mr Jones. Would you mind if I introduced you to him?" '

If this is done properly, most guests will be flattered and will gladly be introduced to you, at which point you say: 'Hello, Mr Jones. I'm John Timperley, a specialist in [...] I hope you don't mind Angela, our receptionist, bringing you over, but I've found to my cost in the past that I spend most of my time on these occasions looking at people's name badges! I'm very glad you could make it today.'

If you have other people with you at this point you would introduce them too, saying, 'Can I introduce you to ...?' Then, if you know it, give the job title or area of specialisation of the person you've just been talking to and a bit about what you were talking about, for example: 'Can I introduce you to Terry Holding? Terry is finance director of A. & V. Holdings, one of my engineering sector clients. We were just talking about whether the recession in the US is likely to have significant impact here.'

In this way, in the space of less than 30 seconds, you could have explained your rationale for having your guest brought to you, introduced your existing conversation partner and brought your new guest right up to speed with your topic of conversation – hopefully one on which they will have a view. (If not, you'll need to change tack to their interests later.)

If the function is not one which you are hosting it's more likely that the reception desk personnel will only agree to telling you when your 'target' contact has arrived and pointing them out to you. That's fine. This action alone has saved you all that time wandering the room surreptitiously peering at name badges (and not all functions have name badges anyway). You would then go into your normal introduction routine when a suitable opportunity presented itself.

What colour are you?

Once they get their teeth into how much more professional they can be in organising themselves to meet the people they want to meet, my clients often get very scientific about the approach. Here are a few organisational tips you may wish to try, each with its own pros and cons:

- Colour code guest badges into clients, 'hot' prospects and others. You could put a spot of coloured felt-tip pen in the top corner of the badge, for example. This is a good way for the hosts to know which category the person they are talking to fits into, which is valuable up to a point, but has the severe downside that you'll need an answer to the question: 'Why have I got a blue spot on my badge and his is red?' You don't want to appear mercenary by sorting the clients and hot prospects from the rest, and someone who feels 'downgraded' simply by the colour of the spot on their badge will be upset.

- A more subtle way of achieving the same result (although sharp-eyed guests may still ask the same question) is to use a different typeface or permutation of capitals and lower case to differentiate between the groups of contacts. For example, you could put all client names in capitals, but hot prospects in initial capitals only. Other guests may have both their name and their company in capitals.

Host a party within a party

In the right venue and with a sizeable guest list (more than 50), one of the very best approaches to meeting the people you want to meet is this: instead of just having a single refreshment point for tea and coffee, have four, preferably one in each corner of the room. Allocate an appropriate number of hosts to a particular point and then divide your guests into four sets in a way that is logical to you – by type of organisation, job function, sector, and so on. You now have four sets of hosts and guests.

As an example, a computer services company I worked with had at one refreshment point:

4 hosts
8 existing clients
4 targets (people you would like as clients)
4 other guests

They colour coded these people's badges quite deliberately and boldly, and on arrival the receptionist told them that they were at the green coffee point.

What's the advantage of this approach? There are several:

- You break a large guest population down into a manageable size, creating a party within a party.

- You select those people you wish to be in your party for your own contact-making and business-development purposes.

- You can find out the latest news about your guests much more easily, because you have a smaller number to handle.

- You can get endorsement from your clients when you are talking to target contacts and they will see the rapport you have with your clients. Your clients can be your very best salespeople.

- As long as the refreshments are replenished properly, there's never a big queue.

- It's much easier to introduce nearby colleagues and generally create a group 'feel', particularly if you've selected guests for your group on the basis of their interests or job roles.

There is also a group psychology about 'belonging'. While no one said that guests can't wander wherever they want in the room, you'll find that 'group norms' apply and people tend to stay together. No one likes to be the odd one out and wear a green badge in a red area!

This approach works well in a pre- and post-seminar situation where the green group who met before the seminar will tend to get back together at the same point for refreshments afterwards. This gives hosts the opportunity to circulate among guests, asking what they thought of the occasion and gaining permission to stay in touch where appropriate.

The approach works less well at cocktail-type functions where people are present for a couple of hours and may simply wish to mingle throughout the room. Nevertheless, the organisational rationale for adopting it is a good one and guests do welcome the feeling of a 'home' base.

The Room Worker's Toolkit

Every profession has its tools of the trade and networking is no different. A plumber's bag will contain all sorts of wrenches, washers, pliers and other devices to deal with all situations, while a doctor's case will have a stethoscope, blood pressure kit and essential pills, bandages and potions. Here we'll cover the tackle a connector needs to use to be truly effective. We've explored the uses of some of these items already, but now let's put them into the context of the connector's 'must haves'.

There are only six key items, but each has its own vital role to play in helping you to achieve your goal of connecting with the right individuals. As you'll see, they are mainly used in the business networking context but are adaptable for purely social situations too.

Business cards – your mini long-term advertisement

We talked about the power of business cards earlier, so we won't cover that ground again. This is about making sure that you have them in your 'toolkit' in the same way that a doctor would not dream of leaving home without a stethoscope.

Business cards are a permanent reminder of who you are and what you do, and double up nicely as a mini notepad on which to jot comments and agreed actions. But they are no use to you in your desk drawer when you are out at a function, or in your briefcase in the cloakroom when you are at a reception. You need them with you at all times. That means checking *before* you go that you have sufficient for the occasion. They may be in your wallet, in a special card case or in your suit pocket, but wherever you normally keep them, make sure that you are fully stocked. Running out of cards is like a doctor running out of essential tablets. It doesn't look professional or engender feelings of trust and competence.

Amateurs have dozens of reasons why they haven't any cards to give out:

'I've just given my last one away.'

'I'm having them redone.'

'Would you believe it, they are in my other suit. I changed it only this morning.'

Connectors don't have any excuse for not having them, because they've *checked*. By the way, it's a great idea to keep a small supply in the glove compartment of your car, in your briefcase and wallet, and even in a pocket of your sports bag. That way, if you do need to replenish your stock, you have a reserve supply reasonably handy in most circumstances.

Cards can come into play on the social side too. In some circles 'social cards' containing your name, home address and telephone numbers are the accepted norm; in others they aren't. But if you want to be a top connector, get some. It's not pretentious to give your personal details to someone you have met socially rather than in a business context.

Just one obvious word of warning, though: make absolutely sure that you really do want to give your card to a new contact. Not everyone likes to take lots of calls at home or divulge their address to relative strangers. Nevertheless, social cards are great to give to your friends and appropriate acquaintances, particularly if you move home or change contact numbers.

A 4 x 2 inch identity

Have you ever arrived at a business function and found that your name had somehow been missed off the guest list and the organiser did not have a pre-typed name badge for you? Have you then suffered the further indignity of wearing a handwritten one? While the organisers may have done their best to correct the mistake, you somehow feel less of a person than those others in the room with a perfectly typed name badge.

In truth, your credibility has been dented by yours not being the same as everyone else's. And you feel it in your confidence when you introduce yourself. 'I'm global president of Amazon Widgets, Inc., the largest supplier in the United States,' you say, but your handwritten badge somehow chops the legs from under you (and blaming the organisers, though justified, appears a bit weak).

The solution? When the connector is telephoning the organisation for a copy of the guest list (next on our toolkit agenda) they'll also check that their name and company details are correct. It's a simple ten-second job that makes sure that they look the part.

And just to be on the safe side, the champion connector will also have their own badge with them! Many organisations these days issue their hosts with classy-looking but inexpensive plastic or metal badges containing their name and organisation logo. A serious connector will have half a dozen made up with their name on and, like their business cards, keep them handy. If, for whatever reason, a handwritten card is the only option despite their call to check (it does happen), then they can use their own.

No fuss, and totally professional, because they have a contingency plan that works.

Who's coming?

The guest list is a critical item in the connector's toolkit. It's their blueprint for the function, their guide to the contact-making opportunities available.

If your own organisation is hosting the function then obtaining a list isn't much of a problem. If it's someone else's event, it's more difficult – but only slightly. All you do is pick up the phone and say: 'Hello, this is John Timperley, I'm due to attend the [function] on Wednesday and just thought I'd have a quick check to make sure you received my confirmation. You have? Good. By the way, some people find the spelling of my name a bit tricky. It's TIM-PER-LEY. OK, great. I'm looking forward to it. By the way, you wouldn't happen to have a guest list you could fax or email to me, would you? I was just wondering who else might be there.'

By the time you get to asking for the guest list you'll probably have built some rapport with your telephone conversation partner. I normally mention some of the misspellings of my name as they check through the list. 'You wouldn't believe it, but I've had Tipperary, Timpoli, Tripperley, Timpani and even been called Tim Pearly before now,' I'll say … and they're all true!

Unless there's a very good reason why you can't have the guest list (and sometimes there is), most organisations will let you have a copy. And that's your chance to use it, professionally, as a way to focus your contact-making efforts.

On the social side you could always telephone your host, if you know them well enough, for a brief rundown of who is going so that you will feel more comfortable about the occasion and can dress appropriately.

Intelligence that makes the difference

A piece of information which took a manager in an accounting practice five minutes to locate and two minutes to read set him on the road to accelerated partnership. Here's how he did it.

As part of the firm's host team for an accounting update seminar, he'd been allocated a 'target' contact to speak to at the event who was MD of a printing company. As part of his research he'd had a quick look at the company's accounts and logged on to the Reuters database to find out the latest news on the company.

A three-paragraph story in a specialist printing journal reported that the company had recently made a £5m acquisition of another business in the sector. Not very big, not very newsworthy – but that piece of information was to transform that accountancy practice's relationship with their target contact.

When the manager met the MD at the accounting update function, after some initial pleasantries and social conversation, he said, 'How's the acquisition going?' Visibly taken aback that the manager should know about the small acquisition, the printing company MD went on to tell him some of the positives and negatives of the situation.

More importantly, when he got back to his office the MD told all of his senior managers about the accountancy firm down the road that was really 'on the ball'. The result? In very short order the accountants were asked to provide a quote for the company's audit and tax work (which they successfully negotiated). The printing company has further expanded to become one of the firm's most valued clients – and all because of five minutes' research and a three-paragraph news story.

That's the power of intelligence. It's the difference between saying 'What does your company do'? (the no research approach) and ' How's the recent acquisition going?' I've no need to ask you which question you think is going to impress most.

A host's briefing on who's who and what's what

If you are hosting a function, make sure that you are organised in advance.

In the social context, even if it's just you and your partner hosting at home, have a chat about who's going to be responsible for what – the food, the drink, the entertainment, the clearing of dishes, even the washing up. It's too late on the night to be arguing over the dinner table about who should be doing what. Of course it happens, and it's probably happened to you. So plan in advance. Lessen the risk of misunderstanding and strife, and maximise your opportunity to connect with your guests in a convivial atmosphere.

The business parallel to this is a formal hosts' briefing. While you are unlikely to be worrying about who's making the food and scrubbing the dishes, you should be considering who will be looking after whom, who wishes to meet which guests and what roles you will play (if any). Will someone meet and greet? Will someone be responsible for drinks? Is anyone to say a few words, and when? Who will be in charge of providing key information on the guests' backgrounds and latest business activities? I could go on. Much depends on the size and nature of the event, but the message should be clear. Leave out the hosts' briefing and you leave everything to chance; it's a gamble connectors prefer not to take.

'I'll jot that down, if I may...'

Capturing information on what you've agreed to do for a contact you've just met can be done in a couple of ways. One way is to write on the back of their card, thereby linking what you are to do with the person's details. Make sure you have their permission to do this, though. A second and perhaps more elegant approach is to keep a very small high-quality notepad and pen with you at all times. Any good stationer can provide one about the size of a very slim cigarette-box or even smaller. I've seen silver-cased ones with a small integral pen. A notepad is ideal for use at a truly social function where it may not be 'good form' to ask for a card.

Writing down key details of what you've agreed shows that you are serious about your networking and your commitment. You simply say: 'I'll just jot that down, if I may, so that I don't forget.' Then you whip out your mini notepad and capture the information. At an appropriate time after the event (the same day or evening is best for recall), note down any additional information that is relevant to your longer-term connecting goals with that person – their likes or dislikes, the main points of your conversation, and so on.

So, we've now worked the room and had lively and interesting conversations with several new contacts. We've developed rapport with some people we would like to meet again. What do we do now to strengthen the initial bond? Let's look at follow-up techniques.

CHAPTER 6

Building the Bond

Y OU'VE HAD A REALLY good conversation or meeting with someone and identified some ways in which you or others may be able to help them. What do you do next?

Whether your discussion has been with someone in your workplace, a potential client or simply someone you would like to get to know better, the basic rule applies: be proactive! You can't strengthen the initial rapport if you do nothing about it. In fact, as time goes by, you and the conversation will move further back in your contact's mind. Indeed, if you take the coy approach and wait for them to reconnect with you, you could be dead and buried before anything happens! Often people don't like to be the first to start building on an initial relationship for no other reason than they have other things on their mind, or are busy or shy, but when *you* take the initiative they are delighted you have done so. So take that minor risk of rejection and follow up your initial contact quickly and effectively.

Follow-up Techniques That Build Relationships – and Business

This is the area of networking where great connectors excel in a polished and non-intrusive way. The type of follow up they use depends on the circumstances, of course, but there are some tried and tested ways that you can consider. Treat them as a 'menu' to refer to, and select those dishes that feel right for the level of relationship you have generated with your contact.

Debrief

If you are part of a host team at a business function, get together after the event to compare notes and find out who met who and who has agreed to do what for whom. If you've worked the room successfully as a team you'll be surprised at the amount of information you'll have gathered. Coordinate your follow-up actions accordingly.

Send a personal note

These are great for thanking people for hosting social functions. Write them by hand for a personal touch if your writing looks good. But you don't have to restrict your thanks to the host. Send notes to others as well, linked specifically to your conversations and what you said you would do, for example:

Graham

It was good to see you again on Friday and great to catch up on the news. I've checked my diary and can do that golf game anytime the last two weeks of September – any good for you?

Let me know when you have a minute.

Yours

Tim

A note like this literally takes two minutes and can really help to cement a relationship. There are lots of 'thank you' cards on the market or blank ones for your own messages. Why not buy a stock of them and keep some in your office, your briefcase and at home so that you'll always have a few handy? Pen a quick note when you meet someone whose actions are worthy of a formal 'thanks'. It could be anything from organising the meeting and contributing to the results to the new lead or the new assignment. Find ways to subtly but tangibly say thanks and you'll be repaid a hundredfold in good will. Everyone likes their efforts to be recognised.

Respond by email

Modern technology makes it even easier to fire off a quick note of thanks or to follow up on specific points. An informal medium, email is great if you want to be low key but quick with your response.

Send a formal letter

On the other hand, a formal letter of appreciation will sometimes be the right tool for the job. It adds gravitas and an air of substance to your follow up.

Make a phone call

Writing is good, but so too is a well-timed telephone call. A call to the host of a function the following day to say 'well done' and how much you enjoyed the function, is a top connector's tactic. It shows stature and interest – and sometimes even brings opportunities to the surface as a follow on to the event.

Calling contacts you've met and agreed a follow-up action with is also a fantastic technique – if done properly. Unless you've promised to call the very next day, though, think twice about doing so. You don't want to seem over-eager and pushy – as if they are the only contact you have. Better to wait a couple of days. It then appears that they were quite high up your agenda but you, rightly, needed to deal with other priority matters first. Clearly, though, if you leave it too long to call not only do you come across as disorganised or disinterested, but they'll probably have forgotten you! Get the balance right.

Send articles/clippings and relevant information

This is both a short- and a long-term tactic for building relationships. While it is useful to send your company brochure and other corporate literature to your contacts, experienced connectors go one better. They know that sending third-party information relevant to their contact's role and interests delivers a much clearer message of their own interest.

For example, if your contact expressed a keen interest in fast cars and said that they owned a Porsche themselves, you would send them the article you've just seen in *Time* magazine on the latest model and how it has road tested. But don't overdo it. Just fax or post it with a handwritten message at the top saying something like: 'I just saw this and thought you might find it interesting if you've not seen it already. All the best, Simon.'

The same could apply to any topic – the latest trends in globalisation in the *Financial Times*, the *Wall Street Journal*'s review of the world's best businesses, the colour pull-out of this season's New York Yankees. Anything goes. If your contact is really interested in it, send it.

However, don't do it too regularly unless they specifically ask you to. And don't make any notes you send too elaborate. Keep them short and to the point. Avoid the 'apple for the teacher' mentality – it can backfire.

Invite them to future events

You really start to build a bond with people when you've met them three or four times and shared some experience of working or socialising together. So think about what events or activities they may be interested in and plan a programme of invitations.

At all times ask yourself 'Why would they come? What's in it for them?' This will help you to avoid sending generic invitations to occasions they are not particularly interested in and risking rejection.

Once you are happy that they would be interested in your suggestion, plan it properly and invite them at least six weeks in advance. Busy people have full diaries and may turn down your invitation simply because they don't have a slot in their calendar. Minimise this risk by being early with your invitation – it shows professionalism.

Remember, it takes three or four meetings or shared experience to really develop a relationship. What's your next step with your fledgling contact going to be?

Ask to see their operations

Taking a real interest in your contact and their business is important in building a connective relationship. After all, how can you expect to help if you don't understand them and their business?

One great way of finding out more and building rapport is to express an interest in visiting their office, site or factory to see how things work. Then you'll have something to add in the area of 'benchmarking' – a fancy name for comparing how they do things with others in a similar situation – particularly if you have experience in their sector or type of business.

Offer to introduce someone who can help

In the course of your discussions an obvious business opportunity may be apparent – but it won't always be for you. If appropriate, offer to introduce your conversation partner to one of your contacts who can help. Be sure though, that your contact can be absolutely relied on to deliver, otherwise you'll be blamed (rightly) for introducing someone who's caused problems rather than solved them.

Invite them back

In the business context, this could take the form of inviting your contact to view your facility or meet some of your colleagues – maybe specialists in specific areas relevant to your contact's needs. You could do it over an informal lunch or dinner, for example. A chat over food is a great way to share ideas and strengthen relationships.

Do them a favour – and meet their objectives

One of the very best things a connector can do is to help their contacts to achieve their objectives. This means putting yourself in your contact's position and doing them a favour of some kind … with no expectation of it being returned.

This is a critical aspect of the connectors' mindset – just trying to assist the other person for the benefit it can provide to them. The personal reward comes partly in the giving and, surprisingly often, from opportunities generated directly from the contact or indirectly through referrals they are able to give. Sometimes you will give far more than you get back, other times the reverse will be true. But to put yourself into the game in the first place you must 'give' first in order to 'get' later.

Remembering Names and Faces Easily

Have you ever felt a fool because you've forgotten the name of the business contact you were introduced to only seconds before? Ever got annoyed because you couldn't remember the telephone number of a key contact and you've forgotten your little black book as well? Ever had a great idea, not written it down and promptly forgotten it? Of course you have!

Our lack of retention means that we are wasting valuable time constantly relearning things we should already know. Tests prove that most of us forget 90 per cent of the names of people we've just met, and at least 95 per cent of phone numbers given to us.

The vast majority of us have an average memory and are using, at most, 10 per cent of its capacity. Studies by psychologist Mark Rosenweig concluded that if we fed in ten new items of information *every second* for a lifetime, the average brain would be only half full. Memory problems, he says, are not caused by the capacity of our brain but by our management of the remembering process.

The truth for most of us is that our memory is lazy and unless we have developed memory techniques which help us to use it properly, we are nowhere near as good as we could be. We tend to keep information in our brains for the shortest possible time and our memory is literally like a sieve.

The problem, though, is not our memory, it's our *recall*. We simply can't recall the bulk of the information our memory has stored away for us. Why?

TRY THIS

If a beautiful woman dressed only in a green thong came up to you on a packed commuter train, kissed you full on the lips for 10 seconds and slapped you in the face as hard as she could afterwards, do you think you would remember that for the rest of your life? Yes? Then why can't you remember the first sentence of this section? (Test yourself!)

The problem is, as Henry Hazlitt put it, 'Our thoughts are so fleeting that no device for trapping them should be overlooked.' He advocated giving your memory a metaphorical 'slap in the face'. Can you visualise that? Imagine slapping your memory – literally, to make it do something (like a jockey slaps a horse to make it run faster). If you can 'see' that picture, you're using the technique that all memory experts use – it's called 'ridiculous association'. A ridiculous picture helps to create effective attention, and it is this that causes you to notice and retain the thing you want to remember.

Think again about what happened to you on the train a moment ago. Why did you remember it? Things like that simply don't happen, it was a ridiculous scenario. It also had action in it, and feeling (kiss and pain ... whatever else is up to your imagination!) It would have been an even stronger memory if the image you had of the woman was larger than life (8 feet tall with attributes to match) – or there were 100 of them all lining up to do the same thing to you. Can you see it?

The secret to a good memory is using your gift of imagination and having the systems in place to make facts memorable.

Why memorising names and faces is important

A good memory gives you the edge. Others in your organisation or business circles probably have had the same education and training as you, and are exposed to the same information on a daily basis. How, then, can you get ahead? Using your memory better is one sure way.

Every experienced connector knows that they have lost a piece of potential business at one time or another through forgetting a contact's name or some key item of relevant information. Kicking oneself after the event may help relieve the feelings of frustration, but it won't retrieve the lost opportunity.

Also gone forever is anything that we do not make a strong enough association with in our mind. And the problem for many organisations and their employees is not just the vitally important social (and business-winning) aspects of remembering names, faces and company information, it is the time taken revisiting information that could (should?) have been committed to memory – telephone numbers, key contacts and their positions, sales and financial figures, the location of reports, and so on. You know the score.

IN PRACTICE

Consider the moral of this story told by David Thomas, one of the best ever memory experts. It's about a rookie stockbroker going for a new job at a top City firm. The competition for the role was intense. No doubt past record, personality and potential were all being taken into account when the candidates were wheeled in.

But the rookie got the job, hands down, no question. Why? Because he had memorised (easily, in half an hour) the names of the firm's major clients, its board members and their specialisms and key facts about the firm and its vision of the future, facts that were available to anyone.

He amazed the panel with his knowledge (he knew more than some of them!) and came across as a hugely intelligent, highly motivated and committed individual whose talents would be a great asset to their business. All due to half an hour's (enjoyable) mental exercise.

Your memory could be your greatest influencing asset too. Are you taking the time to use it? Let's focus on one of the key aspects, remembering people's names.

Putting an indelible name to a face

'Oh, I know your face but just can't place your name.' Have you ever had to say this? If you are like most people, it will have happened many times. It's not a pleasant rapport-building experience. No one likes to be forgotten.

Almost invariably, it's the person's name that's escaped you, not their face. Why? Because most of us are visual rather than auditory creatures. Things we *see* register more deeply than things we *hear*. When we meet someone we always see their face (unless it's a very dark disco) but often only hear their name (if it's in a disco you've no chance of hearing anything!). And that's the very reason why the majority of us, when we happen to meet our conversation partner again, utter the ageless line: 'I recognise your face, but I can't remember your name.'

Sometimes such a *faux pas* is more than embarrassing – it can hurt your relationship building and your business. It can even cost you money. (Would a potential client hire you if you can't remember their name, or your competitor, who clearly is on first-name terms?)

Tricks don't always stick

As forgetting names is such a common problem, people have tried umpteen ways to 'trick' people into giving their name again. Most of these are fundamentally flawed, but for the fun of it let's eavesdrop on a couple ...

Joanne met a business acquaintance whose name she could not recall, so she asked in desperation: 'How do you spell your surname again?' 'The only way it can be spelled,' came the incredulous retort. 'J-O-N-E-S.' (Ouch!)

A friend of mine, Paul, used another technique – until it backfired. He used to remember names by 'rhyming association' and was very proud of his technique until he met his son's teacher Mrs Hummock, a pleasant but rather stout lady with a large stomach. Paul made the obvious mental connection of Hummock with stomach and carried on his business, safe in the knowledge that he wouldn't forget that name in a hurry. At parents evening a few months later he met the teacher again, glanced at her protruding belly and proceeded to call her Mrs Kelly!

Before we get into memory techniques, some of which are more effective than others, just reflect on the fact that Cyrus, the Greek general, using a memory technique, could remember the names of thousands of the soldiers and villagers in his care. How? We'll see later. In the meantime consider some of these techniques:

- In elegant circles, one favourite way of pretending you didn't forget someone you should have remembered is simply to ask the person what their name is. It's more crafty than it appears. If they tell you their first name, you say: 'Oh, I wouldn't forget *that*, it's your surname I meant.' Naturally, if the person volunteers their surname first, you can then turn it round and say you know *that*, but what you were after was their first name. (Told you it was crafty!) Using this sneaky technique you get the person's full name and it appears that you have only forgotten one. Your downfall comes, however, when the person gives their full name straight away – then you've no tricks to pull and it looks as if you have forgotten their name and have brazenly come out and asked for it again (which you have!)

- Some people I've known use the alphabet or first initial method and make a fantastic effort to retain only the initial of the person's name. The technique works on the principle that by only having to remember the initial you free your brain of all unnecessary information, and recalling the initial helps you to recall the entire name. Try it if you want, but my experience is that you can forget the initial just as easily as you do the name – and if you do happen to remember the initial you're still not sure whether your acquaintance was Anne, Annette or Anthea!

- Without a doubt, writing names down on paper can help recall – some experts suggest compiling a 'memory book' by writing down the names of every person you meet and want to remember. It sounds plausible and it's better than nothing, but it's less than foolproof when you are looking directly into the face of your new acquaintance and racking your brain for the name to associate with the face. And I don't think flicking through the pages of your notebook, surreptitiously or otherwise, until the face and name 'click' is the fast-track way to rapport either.

- More practical 'on-the-spot' techniques include associating a person's name with someone you know already. So, if you've just met Anne Carr and you already have a friend called Anne you are likely to remember your new acquaintance's name more readily than if you know no one by that name. The only problem is, when you see Anne Carr, will her face conjure up your friend Anne's name? Sometimes yes, sometimes no.

- The same applies to people who remind you of others by their demeanour, looks, smile, voice, humour or whatever. So, Jack, whom you've just met, distinctly resembles your pal Ron from school. So far so good, but there's grave danger that when you next see Jack he'll immediately remind you of your old school chum … and you'll call him Ron!

If you start playing the tricks just mentioned, you're indulging in Russian roulette with social embarrassment. It may work for a while, but sooner or later it will blow up in your face, usually at the least opportune moment.

So what's the answer? It depends on how much effort you want to put into this critical aspect of connecting, but if Cicero could do it, why can't you? He had a system that we're going to explore some more.

IN PRACTICE

Not too long ago a cloakroom attendant in a swish New York nightspot became one of its best attractions simply because of her memory. She never issued a ticket for hats and coats left with her. Instead she would remember which item of apparel belonged to whom (and it's said that she never made a mistake in giving any-one the wrong items).

Her secret of this 'superhuman' feat was a memory technique she developed to associate the hat, coat and other paraphernalia with their owner's face. We are going to adapt that technique to remember names.

Harry Lorraine, the great memory expert, also tells the story of a bellboy of a large hotel in the southern United States who has gained a similar reputation. Whenever someone checks into the hotel who has been there even once before, this bellboy addresses them by name. At the time Harry told this tale the bellboy was well on the way to saving enough money out of his tips to buy the place!

The cloakroom attendant and the bellboy prove a couple of things. First, people love to be remembered. It makes them feel important. And second, they'll even pay for the privilege.

Spurred on by these heart-warming – and financially rewarding – effects of remembering, let's delve a lot deeper into how to do it. But first here's a shocker for you …

Learning to listen

The world's top memory expert at the moment, David Thomas, told me this gem – and it's probably the most important point of all. The main reason that most people forget a name is that they *never remembered it in the first place!* What's more, they may not have even *heard* the name!

How often have you been introduced to someone in this fashion: 'John, I'd like you to meet Mrs Ste ... ve ... ge?' Instead of the name, all you hear is a mumbled, muffled sound. Maybe it's because the person introducing you doesn't know the woman's name either, or the environment you are in is noisy and you simply didn't catch it. Either way, if you are like most people you'll think that you'll never meet this person again, so you say 'Nice to meet you' and never bother to get the name right. You may then spend a little while talking to this person, or even all night, and finally say goodbye still not knowing their name. You can hardly ask their name halfway through the conversation and the best time to have done it – right at the start of your chat – is way behind you now.

So, the first rule for remembering names is an obvious one: *be sure you heard it in the first place.* You see, the odds are that you will remember a person's face when you see it again, but you'll only *hear* the name and, as we've seen, our hearing recall is not normally as strong as our sight recall. If you didn't hear it properly, ask your introducer or your new friend to say it again. And if you're not sure of the pronunciation or the spelling, have a go yourself and check. Ask: 'How do you spell that?' for a name that is unusual or could have a variety of spellings (Smith, Smyth, Smythe, or Brown, Browne or Braun, for example). It's a good conversation starting-point, it demonstrates your interest and, critically for this purpose, helps you to get a better fix on the person and the name.

This technique is particularly useful for connectors with international contacts whose unfamiliar names may be difficult to remember, pronounce and spell! So take an interest – if you didn't hear it properly say so and ask for it to be repeated, have a go at the pronunciation and check the spelling, all of which will help enormously to embed the name firmly in your memory. It will also flatter your conversation colleague that you are interested enough in them to want to get their details correct. Now that's what I call a 'win–win' situation.

IN PRACTICE

Harry Lorraine, the memory man from whom these techniques have been borrowed, tells the story of how one of his several excellent books on the subject came to be published.

He had spoken to a publisher, James Fell, when they met socially and Mr Fell said that he would mull over the possibility of asking Harry to pen a book about his techniques.

Five months later, after meeting thousands of people (Harry did a nightly show where he remembered the names of *everyone* in the audience), Harry was performing at a charity breakfast when a man approached him and asked if he remembered him.

Because of the memory connection he had made nearly half a year before, Harry could immediately say, 'Of course, Mr Fell.' At which Mr Fell confessed that he had visited the performance to test Harry to make sure that he was as good as he claimed. The book deal, and several more, ensued.

To embed a name in your memory, when talking to a new person repeat their name as often as is appropriate during the conversation. But be careful here – too generous a sprinkling of the name will make you sound false and insincere, which is the exact opposite of what you are trying to achieve. Just use their name whenever and wherever it fits. Each time you repeat it, it will have the effect of dropping another coin into your memory bank. At the very least, use it when you say goodbye. Something like this will do: 'Jean, it's been great to talk to you. I hope we'll meet again soon.'

Don't worry if you feel uncomfortable doing this at first. After three or four conversations, using people's names in this way will become second nature. What's more, you'll be doing what experienced connectors do to make their conversation partners feel that they are really interested in them.

Champion connectors take this to a higher level using techniques like those Cicero employed centuries before. Here's how.

First they use all of the basic building-blocks highlighted earlier. They:

- Make sure they hear the name in the first place.

- Spell it or have their acquaintance spell it if it's unusual.

- Comment on any unusual aspect or if it is similar to or the same as that of someone they know already.

- Repeat the name appropriately during the conversation.

- Use the name when they say goodbye.

Some advanced techniques for memorising names

When you think about it, you'll realise that all names can be put into two categories: names that mean something and names that don't.

Names that have some meaning include favourites like Baker, Carpenter, Butcher, Brown, Fox, Harper, Taylor, Field, Green, Whiteside, Carr – there are hundreds of them, but you'll have got the picture by now.

Then there are names that don't appear to have any meaning at all. Take these pulled at random from the telephone directory as examples: Mattinson, Layton, Buckley, Hipkin, Kelly, Mather, Pascarelli, Schenkel, Sayeed, Waheed.

In fact there is a subset of the 'no meaning' category which includes people or places you know with the same name, examples of which would be Travolta, Gibson, Cruise, Melbourne, Pavarotti, Washington, Lincoln, Gandhi and Churchill.

All of these names will probably conjure up an image in your mind's eye as you read them ... and that is exactly the core of the memory technique you are about to experience. That is, in order to remember the name you must make it mean something to you. The difficult category is the one where the names mean nothing to you – but even that's not hard when you realise that no matter how strange a name sounds it can always be broken down into a substitute word or thought.

By 'substitute word or thought' I mean just think of a word or phrase that sounds as much like the name as possible. Let's have a go at some examples from the earlier list to get us in the mood.

- **Mattinson** could become 'Mat-in-son'. Picture in your mind's eye a mat being swallowed whole by your son (it doesn't matter whether you have a real son or not, we're using our imagination here). See clearly the mat going down. Be ridiculous with your image, that's what your memory loves! When you can see it clearly, move on to this:

- **Layton** could bring to mind the image of yourself lying on top of a ton weight, or, better still, a ton weight lying on top of you. If you don't fancy these two images, try picturing yourself 'laying' a path of thousands of ton weights that stretches for miles (Lay-ton). Feel the weight, experience the size in your mind's eye … That's Layton done.

- **Buckley** (Buckle-E): Imagine your belt buckle is a gigantic 'E' (exaggerate wildly and you'll remember it) or see yourself strapping a buckle around a huge 'E' to restrain it.

Get the idea? Make the images ridiculous, out of proportion, colourful, amusing, scary, weird or sexy and you'll remember them because that's how the brain works. You can easily do the same with first names. Often you can associate the first name with someone you already know with that name. Or, if you don't know anyone, create an appropriate mental image. So Jane could suggest 'chain', John could be 'join' and Mary 'marry'.

At this stage you may be wondering what all this has to do with actually putting names to faces. More of that in a minute, but in the meantime, try creating mental pictures for the other names in the 'no meaning' category. I've dropped in a few suggestions to help.

- Hipkin (Hip and your mother (kin))

- Kelly (Kill 'E')

- Mather (Mother)

- Pascarelli (You pass a car being driven by an 'L' with an 'E' in the passenger seat giving instructions – weird, but it works)

- Schenkel (Shin kill)

- Sayeed (Say-'e' or 'sighed')

- Waheed (Weed, warhead or worried)

You'll see that some names are easier than others to translate into images, but believe me, every name can be if you are creative enough. You'll see that the words and phrases you use don't have to exactly match the names – they are an aid to memory, a stepping-stone to allow you to recall the real name, that's all. So don't get too hung up if you can't find something appropriate for all syllables of a name.

You now have the power to give any name some meaning and are in a position to associate the name with the face in such a way as to remember both. So ...

Go on, be ridiculous!

The best way to do it is a ridiculous one – in fact, the more ridiculous, the better! So, whenever you meet someone new, look at their face and try to find *one* outstanding feature. It could be anything – freckles, a moustache, big lips, small lips, bushy eyebrows, a big nose, moles, dimples, crooked teeth, big ears... The point is that as you are looking for this feature you are taking in the entire face and making yourself be interested in it – and you know by now that interest equals memory.

So far, so good. You're taking in the whole face and looking specifically for one outstanding feature. When you've hit on it you are now ready to associate the person's name with that particular feature. Let's have a go, using some of the names we've already played with. If you thought of different visual images from me, use yours. We all have our own unique ways of seeing things, so your own will be stronger for you than mine.

- **Miss Mattinson has very full lips** I would see myself pulling my son (who has swallowed the mat whole, remember) out of Miss Mattinson's lips. It's a struggle. Can you picture that?

- **Mr Layton has bushy eyebrows** I would see myself lying across those eyebrows, unable to move, as I have a ton weight on my chest (Lay-ton) See it, feel it...

- **Mrs Buckley has a turned-up nose** I would see myself trying to strap a huge 'E' to her nose with a buckle, and I'm pulling it tighter and tighter, which has the effect of turning her nose up even more... Bizarre, I know, but it works. Bet you've remembered it!

So, to summarise, all you need to do once you know your conversation partner's name is to translate it, if necessary, into a substitute word or meaningful phrase and, while your are conversing, search their face for the feature which stands out most to you. Then associate your substitute word or phrase with that feature in a ridiculous way.

Ten seconds to memory

Now you might think that all this is a convoluted way to remember someone's name. But it's like learning to ride a bike – it takes a bit of concentration and trial and error at first, but once you've got the hang of it, it becomes second nature and you'll do it almost without thinking about it – certainly within ten seconds in most cases.

You have a choice, of course – you can go on forgetting names and resort to some of the tricks we saw earlier, or persevere with this approach. It's the one used by champion connectors to be sure that they will retain the name, not just while they are talking to the person, but when they next meet.

You see, the stronger the mental image you form when you link the name with the person's outstanding feature, the longer it remains in your memory, and it will be there for recall when you next happen across them.

For the best long-term results the pros do this: after meeting several people and using the name association technique, they write down the names of the folk they've met that day while recalling the face. Later they'll review the list of names and the face each name is associated with will pop into their mind.

TRY THIS

As a quick exercise, write down five names of your friends, then for each bring up a picture of their face in your mind's eye. Then for each name create an appropriate substitute word or thought and practise associating them with a prominent facial feature.

Recalling the right person's name at the right time may mean a great deal to you in the future. It might be the stepping-stone to a better job, a new contract, a bigger opportunity or a new friendship, all of which will enhance your life. Give the systems a good workout and they'll repay you handsomely.

THE CONNECTOR'S TOOLKIT

When you meet someone you need to give them your full attention. Rather than thinking ahead to what you are going to say next, pay attention to what they are saying. (If you've got your self-introduction off pat, it will be so much easier to focus on your conversation partner.)

At more formal functions such as seminars, conferences and trade shows, the way the pros do it is like this:

- *Hear* the name as the person introduces themselves.

- *See* the name by glancing down at the person's badge.

- *Look* at the name (and other relevant details) on their business card.

- *Review* the card soon afterwards, preferably that evening at the latest, in order to recall the name and other details, and to practise putting the name to the face.

- *Write* the contact's details in an address book if appropriate.

Having a good memory is a major asset for a connector. If you can't remember people, what they do and how you can help each other, you're not making the most of your contact-making opportunities.

What to Do When You've Won the Assignment

Connecting is not only about making new contacts and building your profile, it's about being of great service to those who have given you a new opportunity or assignment. No matter how professional you are and how good you are at what you do, your boss, colleagues and clients are just like you – human. And the more you relate to them person to person, the better and more rewarding your relationships will be.

The bedrock of building a good business relationship in any field is to do an excellent job, but that's only the start. It's crucial that you underpin your work by strengthening that bond with your contacts. Often it's about getting the basics right – those actions that are often forgotten by lesser networkers or those focused on 'business at any price'. Try this formula just as soon as you are given a new assignment or win a new client or customer:

Absorb their issues

Understand their issues quickly. Consider whether there is anything you can do to help over and above your existing new relationship. (We're not talking about doing anything else yet, just understanding their wider position so that you can have informed discussions at an appropriate time.)

Pen a formal 'thanks'

If it's relevant, send a note of thanks to whoever has been responsible for providing the new opportunity for you. It is a courteous act and will get you noticed. While you're at it, promise the highest level of service. Your contact needs to know that they made the right decision in choosing you, and your note starts to put down the foundations of a long-term relationship.

Become a player in their team

Continue to develop a professional but friendly relationship both with your major contact and with their wider team. Remember details about them and really demonstrate that you care about what's going on with them and their area of the business. Build a strong working relationship based on mutual respect and it will pay you back a hundredfold. The odd joke and bit of fun won't go amiss either!

Become known and liked

As soon as you can, request a visit to meet their key people – and chat to others you meet along the way. Tell them how pleased you are to be working alongside them and ask them to let you know if they have any suggestions on how you can do the job better. You need to become known within the organisation – flesh and blood with a name, a face and a personality, not some nebulous figure no one knows. It is easy to sack a nebulous figure but much harder, even if it is justified, to get rid of a genuine 'hands-on' person who is trying to help.

Remember, Remember ...

Winning new business or being offered a new opportunity in your organisation is only the start of the relationship. The big prize comes from nurturing your contacts, identifying with their business and (where appropriate) personal needs and being on hand to help. That's how further opportunities present themselves.

TRY THIS

Test yourself. For your key business contacts or work colleagues do you know their:

- Hobbies and interests.
- Birthday.
- Favourite sport.
- Partner's name, occupation and hobbies.
- Children's names, schools and special talents.

The best connectors do. And that's only the start. Ace connectors may also have a record of the dates they last contacted their client or customer, with one-liners on the subjects covered, the dates key information was sent and copies of relevant bits of news or information which they forwarded to the client for interest!

Strengthen the bond

With this sort of information at their fingertips the connector can, easily and simply, use civil personal touches to further cement a successful working relationship. I'm talking about, for instance, a birthday card, or an email commenting on the contact's sports team's big win, a congratulatory note on their child's successful graduation, a letter inviting them and their spouse to dinner or a corporate function.

All in all, you need the raw data – constantly updated – to create the tools to become a champion connector. It may take time to gather it effectively and sensitively. No one likes the 'questionnaire' approach to their personal lives, but there is no better way to really connect with people in a professional, non-intrusive but very human way.

Ultimately, your business and personal success depends on how devoted you are to the care of your contacts. Are you taking the champion connector's route?

Managing Your Contacts Database

It's not enough to simply have a database of people you've met. It is also necessary to nurture your contacts through keeping in touch, sharing information and giving without receiving. It's not about using people, but about keeping them informed about developments which may be of interest to them but may not always be relevant to you.

It's often later, sometimes never, that a contact gives something back. On the other hand, while some contacts never give anything directly, they may be a great referrer of opportunities to you. If you are networking effectively you could potentially have generated a huge list of names and masses of detail on those people you have met and would wish to retain contact with. To use these lists effectively the details need to be recorded and refreshed.

The type of database you use depends entirely on the type of person you are and the nature of your networking. You may wish to retain a small number of key contacts that meet your networking aspirations. On the other hand, your role may bring you into contact with very many people, all of whom may be valuable to you, or you to them.

You may be interested in computers, for example, and welcome the opportunity to use one of the fantastic contact and sales tracking databases such as 'Act' by Interact, or you may be a personal organiser fan and use that device. Alternatively, you may prefer the tried and tested little black address book or a Rolodex card system.

In a way the type of system doesn't really matter. The key thing to ask yourself is: 'When will I need access to the information in my system and will my present approach allow me to get it when I need it?' A desk-based card system is of little use if you spend most of your time on the road, and you're hardly likely to persevere with a computer-based one if computers don't form part of your normal working life.

The key action for a connector is to keep his database fresh and the best way to do this is to keep in regular touch with your contacts so that you know of any changes in their circumstances. Those phone calls, emails, letters and invites to functions are not just the route to the cleansing of a database, though, but to great relationships as well. They are your highway to being in the right place at the right time when opportunities arise.

To make the most of these opportunities, you also need to know the rules of social and business etiquette.

CHAPTER 7

Business Etiquette

YOU CAN'T BE a complete connector if you don't follow the rules of social and business etiquette. We're not talking here about convoluted customs and ridiculous aristocratic practice, but good business manners, actions that show you care and reveal your maturity as a business person.

Manners are simply a vehicle for getting along with other people. Good manners smooth the way for relationships; bad ones jar. Manners can make a tremendous difference to the way people view you. It pays to know the correct business etiquette.

Being the Good Host

There are many tried and tested ways to entertain for business. Some of these may appeal – all have their merits:

- A 'quickfire' breakfast meeting.

- Lunch, in a restaurant, a private room or at your office.

- Coffee in a hotel lobby or at your (or their) office.

- Dinner in the usual places or at your home.

- Watching or participating in sport.

- A trip to the theatre for a bit of culture, with food before or afterwards.

- All manner of other 'corporate hospitality'.

Despite the range of entertaining options, eating out is probably the most used form of business entertainment. It's as informal or formal as you want, the choice of venue and cuisine is vast (and ever increasing), but the social protocols to make everything run smoothly have been around for years. Experienced networkers know what can go wrong in these circumstances and how best to pave the way for a thoroughly pleasant exchange. Let's start by having a look at some dining and cocktail-party tips.

Restaurant tips

Dining in a restaurant can be either great for networking or a relationship-destroying disaster. Improve the odds in your favour by:

- Checking what kind of food your guest likes and choosing a restaurant that meets their needs, not yours. (Not everyone likes seafood and it's too late once you're in Crabby Bill's to find out your guest is allergic to anything from the sea.)

- Be clear from the outset who is picking up the bill. It avoids embarrassing discussions later, shows professionalism and gives your guest the comfort of knowing where they stand.

- If you are the host, make two *essential* phone calls on the day: one to the restaurant to reconfirm the reservation you made initially and the other to your guest to make sure that they can still make it. Confirm the time and tell them how much you are looking forward to meeting up.

- If you haven't agreed to meet in the reception area of the restaurant and you are the first to arrive, the correct protocol is to ask the head waiter to show you to your table. But don't, whatever you do, start eating the rolls or order your meal. Social etiquette says that the table should be untouched before the other person arrives.

- It's normal routine to have a drink before the meal – just one, though. Two is considered bad form. If you're having wine with the meal and you are on a budget and have agreed to pick up the bill, be proactive by pointing to one of the lesser or mid-range wines and saying: 'How about one of these?' If you're having lunch, consider the option of ordering wine by the glass, not the bottle. Not everyone wants to drink at lunchtime and you may be in the embarrassing position of having nearly half a bottle left. The elegant solution is *not* to down the lot yourself!

- You can help your guest in the same way with the choice of meal. Tell them about the special dishes of the restaurant and tell them what you're going to have. That way they will feel comfortable ordering something in your price range. If you want them to have anything they fancy on the menu, say so upfront. It dissolves the hesitancy and awareness of making the 'right' choice.

- A professional touch is to make sure that your guest is served first. It shows you care. Later, ask their opinion of the food and whether everything is OK. Not only is this courteous, but it shows you are interested in them and their well-being, not just the content of the business conversation.

- Don't jump straight into a business discussion as soon as your bum hits the chair. Not only is it bad manners, it's also bad business sense. Getting down to the nitty gritty too soon makes you look aggressive and unfeeling. Ease into the conversation with small talk and find out a little more about what's happening in your guest's world. It builds rapport, adds context and helps you to create a foundation for a meaningful discussion later.

Dinner-party tips

If you are organising a formal dinner for a few folk, or even hundreds, the same key fundamentals apply:

- Send out the invitation six to eight weeks in advance and a 'Delighted you can attend' reminder note a week or so before – this flushes out the people who may have forgotten or who may have other commitments looming and serves to put everyone else 'under starter's orders' so that they are properly prepared.

- If you can arrange it, round tables of eight guests are best for conversation. Round tables also avoid any protocol problems of who sits at the head of the table. Tables of 10 or 12 are too big to allow you to speak to the person opposite and at the far end. Oblong or long tables often mean that you can only speak comfortably to four or five people without talking across others' conversations.

- Make sure everyone knows where they are sitting to avoid a rugby scrum of people at the tables searching for their spot or constant enquires from guests asking whom they are seated next to. The answer is an easily readable table plan. Another way of gaining popularity is to prepare individual cards, each displaying a guest's name and table number – very discreet and very professional.

Being the Delightful Guest

Be the guest who is invited back next time by following these tips:

- Reply to any invitation within a week of receiving it – it helps the host to plan properly. If something crops up and you can't make it, tell them as soon as possible. If something happens on the day and you simply can't get there – for example, a delayed flight or a longer than expected business meeting – make sure you send an apologetic note as soon as you can. It's not only good business etiquette – your thoughtfulness will be noticed, while other non-attendees will be dismissed as 'rude' by the event organisers.

- Always greet your hosts first, before you get a drink and before you get engrossed in conversation with your chums.

- Help your hosts by mingling with the other guests, particularly anyone who looks a little lost or out of the conversation.

- Don't start eating until your host does or, if there is a guest of honour (who should be seated on the host's right), before they do. If your host tells you to start, however, do so. Sometimes by the time a hot starter like soup is out, those served first will be sampling the delights of a cold one!

- The correct social protocol for dinner-table conversation is to talk to guests on either side of you equally. The traditional guidance was to talk to your dinner partner on one side for the first course then switch partners for the next course, then switch back again. This is not easy to do, and the ebb and flow of conversation may take you elsewhere, but the principle remains. So, if you don't want to slight your dining partners, speak to the people on either side of you in equal proportion.

- Make a real point of thanking your hosts at the end of the evening – even if you have to wait in a 'queue' to do so – and back up your verbal thanks with a note just as soon as you can. The best bet is to put pen to paper immediately you get home. A late thanks is almost worse then no thanks at all. It looks as though you had other more important things to do.

Table Manners

Store these tips in your manners 'memory bank':

- Wait for your host to signal you to sit down at the table before taking a seat. Take the napkin from the table and fold it on your lap. (If you need to leave the table during the meal, leave the napkin on your chair, not on the table – your fellow diners don't particularly want to look at what you've spilled!)

- It's protocol not to eat your roll and butter until your meal order has been taken and even then the right way to eat a roll is not to cut it in half with your knife and butter both insides. The elegant way is to break a section off with your fingers and to butter each section as you eat it.

- For cutlery the advice is simple: work from outside in. Cutlery is always set out in logical fashion with the starter implements on the outside and so on through to dessert. Often the dessert spoon and fork will be at the top of the place setting.

- Lean the right way. Trained waiters serve from the left and remove from the right. Help them by moving out of the way as appropriate. It also helps lessen the risk of a dirty fork ending up in your lap.

- If the food is being passed on a platter, take small portions – people watch and won't thank you for taking the 'lion's share'. If the platter has vegetables on it as well, the correct form is to take a small portion of each type, not to shovel your favourite vegetables onto your plate!

- When you haven't finished eating but need a breather or are chatting, put your knife and fork in the 'rest' position (yes, there is one), which means arranging your fork on the left edge of your plate, knife on the right, with the tips meeting in the centre of the upper rim.

- To signal that you have finished a course, put your knife and fork vertically, side by side, on the outer right-hand rim of your plate.

- If a finger bowl is offered to you after eating messy foods, the classy way to do the job is to dip the tips of all your fingers in the water and wipe them on your napkin. Many restaurants provide hot towels following the meal. Here the correct form is to use the towel to wipe your mouth and hands only, not to plunge your face into it or use it to give your ears and neck a good scrub! Have some decorum and use the towel appropriately. When you've finished, put it back on the tray it came on or leave it near your place at the table.

- Yes, you should spoon soup away from you, and hold a piece of chicken or chop in the fingers of one hand at a picnic or barbecue (use a knife and fork if eating it for dinner).

- Yes, you should eat steak by cutting a small piece at a time, not cutting it all up at once (only parents do that for children who are incapable).

- No, you shouldn't eat spaghetti unless you know what you are doing and are armed with a napkin. Splashing bolognese sauce on yourself, the table or, worse, your eating companions is not conducive to the image of a refined connector – and could cost you a fortune in dry-cleaning bills!

- No, you shouldn't shovel peas or other vegetables onto your flat fork. Instead, use your knife or a piece of bread roll to guide them gracefully onto the tines of your fork.

Drinks Form

Can you hold your wine?

Hold your white wine glass or rosé or champagne glass by the stem. The wine has been chilled, so don't spoil it by warming it with your hands. Red wine, however, needs the warmth of your fingers to bring out its flavour, so hold your fingers around the middle of a red wine goblet and 'caress' the wine in your hand.

'Your tiny hand is frozen'

To avoid that cold, clammy handshake, it's a good tip to hold iced drinks in your left hand so that your right hand is free and dry for shaking hands with fellow guests.

'Not for me, thanks!'

If you don't want wine, for example when seated at a dinner, placing two fingers of your right hand on the rim of your glass should be enough to tell the waiter so. But be aware that not all waiters are formally trained – some are students earning an extra crust – and I've had wine poured all over my fingers before now. If necessary, get ready to open your mouth – to tell them 'no'!

The Unwritten Rules of International Etiquette

As business becomes increasingly global we need to raise our level of sensitivity to the cultures with which we interact. Many a connector's good groundwork has been scuppered by an inappropriate gesture through a lack of understanding of a contact's culture, religious beliefs, dietary habits and ways of doing business.

Whether your business is multinational, multicultural or has to work across geographical borders, it is essential to recognise that different rules, manners, attitudes and protocols apply.

IN PRACTICE

Since the German company Daimler Benz hooked up with American giant Chrysler in 1998 in a huge $35 billion merger, major cultural differences have emerged between the two camps. These include differences in, for example:

- **Attitudes to decision-making** An early heated boardroom debate about whether to buy the outstanding stake in the company's loss-making rail system had the Americans demanding it be dumped on grounds of poor performance, while the Germans argued that short-term performance shouldn't be the only criterion for the decision.

- **Approaches to finance** American admiration for German

attention to detail soon faded when they had to deal with 100-page financial reports packed with data instead of their preferred two pages of analysis.

- **Global orientation** The Germans had a far more global and informed approach to world markets.

Will the two cultures gel successfully? Time will tell.

Not all cultures have the same business hierarchy as those of the West, or even your home country. As an example, a Korean employee working in the UK would expect to be told what to do when attending meetings, rather than make decisions. It might take months of adapting to the UK way of working before they could begin to take real responsibility.

In a survey of Asian managers, two-thirds said that connections are more important than strategy for business success in Asia. In China, *guanxi* in essence means 'before we can deal with you, you must be hooked into our circle'. And many Russians still do business on the basis of *blat*, or favouritism, based on personal connections.

In people-oriented corporate cultures like Spain, Portugal and Belgium, people at whatever level of the hierarchy tend to do lots of things at once and as a result they can be easily distracted. They consider a time commitment something to be achieved 'if possible' and often cancel appointments at the last minute. On the other hand, in more project-oriented business cultures like the UK and US, business people have a very strict attitude to time. If you've arranged a meeting you are expected to be there, and on time. Equally, it's often very difficult to see people at short notice because their diary is already pre-booked.

In Saudi Arabia and other Middle Eastern cultures, being late is acceptable, for cultural reasons. You see, if the Saudi businessman you are due to meet is asked for help or advice during his previous meeting, he will see his first priority as resolving the immediate issue. In his culture, it would be seen as highly discourteous to inform the person asking for help that he will deal with it later.

IN PRACTICE

A survey of the workplace behaviour of 144 Asian American managers revealed that they engage less in acts of 'self-disclosure' (volunteering information about themselves) and can appear more aloof than their Western counterparts. It's all in the culture ...

When negotiating an international technology joint venture, US Railway Signals found that its Chinese partners were willing to reduce the productivity of the venture to ensure that all existing employees were involved. The Chinese saw this people issue as their social responsibility, but to the Americans the Chinese lacked the commercial sense they were used to. It's all in the culture ...

Know the business basics

Top connectors recognise that they have an obligation to learn as much as possible about the laws and customs of their international contacts. But that's not all – to be really impressive you need a 'core' of information in your memory bank which proves you are someone worth doing business with.

Such core information includes a knowledge of how the country's government works, the names of its key political parties and leaders, the facts about its key cities, major holidays and feasts, national treasures and major landmarks. In short, you need to be seen to have taken a real interest. Luckily, this is not difficult. There are several competing guides to doing business in almost any area of the world and many countries' overseas trade departments or chambers of commerce provide such 'potted' information.

The important point is that once you have the information, you should use it. Better still, try to get to know your country's government representative for your contact's home territory and quiz them about the unwritten rules of doing business there, such as their ways of negotiating. The conversation could save you a lot of time and money and show that you are an experienced international business person. The more knowledge you have, the more you will avoid unnecessary cultural and business *faux pas*.

Learn the lingo

Of course, the ideal networking plus is to learn your contact's language. But not everyone has the time, or ability, to quickly get up to speed with the business language of a foreign country, so do the next best thing. Pick 20 of the important phrases you will need to get around – simple ones like 'yes', 'no', 'good morning', 'goodnight', 'hello', 'goodbye', 'thank you', 'pleased to meet you' and last but not least, 'how much?' These common phrases – and more if you can – coupled with your knowledge of key aspects of business and politics in their country, will do wonders for your standing in the eyes of your international contacts.

Be the great international host

The next job is to look after your foreign guests properly when you play host. A few thoughtful actions can go a very long way in impressing them and showing that you care. For instance, you could prepare a 'welcome pack' and have it put in your guest's hotel room. Also include a quality guide to your home city and, if you want to really impress, a short note highlighting which pages have really interesting destinations or activities. As always, include a handwritten cover note of welcome. You could also give an appropriate gift – something representative of your home country is usually the safest bet.

Make a fuss of them. Have their photo taken with you, toast them at meals – particularly when other colleagues are present – and always have a bi-lingual dictionary with you. It shows that you are trying, and your effort will be appreciated.

Spoil the spouse

If your contact's spouse/partner is accompanying them on the visit, why not consider a specially arranged schedule so that they will get the best out of their time in your city – and be less inclined to complain if their 'other half' is in business discussions with you?

If there's time, arrange a visit to something of interest. You will know what is appropriate, depending on your relationship with your contact and their understanding of your culture and language.

Check the small print

A word of caution, though: if you are conducting serious negotiations, hire a quality interpreter. They are worth their weight in gold in avoiding misunderstandings, clarifying what everyone is saying and expects, and generally flagging up any woolly areas which could lead to possible dispute somewhere down the line. Whatever you do, don't leave negotiations to be finalised on the basis of a bi-lingual dictionary and a poor understanding of the business language of both parties.

IN PRACTICE

A JP Morgan study found that about 44 per cent of cross-border mergers in Europe failed to add value after three years. Other studies put the figure as high as 60 per cent. A clash of corporate and national cultures is cited as one of the principal impediments to performance.

A report from McKinsey says that an average 15–25 per cent of international assignments fail. Figures rise to as high as 70 per cent for assignments to developing countries. Poor cross-cultural adjustment is seen as one of the major reasons for these figures.

Some international networking no-nos

- Don't take your international visitor to a restaurant featuring their own country's specialities – they usually aren't as good and they eat that type of food at home anyway. Better to try a good restaurant featuring the local delicacies, or maybe even invite them to your own home for a traditional meal.

- Never criticise the government of the other country, or that of your own. It is so easy for a misunderstanding to arise and it may be difficult to dig yourself out of the hole. Unless you are in politics, leave your political opinions at home.

- Don't hug, touch, embrace or kiss people from a culture other than your own unless you are certain of the protocol they would expect. Handshakes aren't always right either, so don't treat this as the all-purpose standby. In the Far East, for example, a slight bow is the order of the day for a greeting and goodbye.

- On the gift side, don't give anything made of cowhide (leather/suede) to a Hindu. The cow is sacred in India. For the same reason don't serve Hindus with beef. Similarly, don't serve pork to a Muslim – it's considered unclean.

- Don't wear all white or send all-white flowers in Asian countries – it's the sign of death and mourning. And on the subject of flowers, don't send red roses to your German hosts because in Germany this flower is reserved for lovers. Unless, of course, that's what you mean to say! Talking of red, in Korea the use of red ink is reserved for recording deaths, but the death colour in Brazil is purple.

- Always hold business cards with both hands when dealing with a contact from the Far East. Never write on the cards in these circumstances – it's the equivalent of desecrating their good name. And never put them in your trouser pocket (the lower the body part, the lower the esteem).

- Always ensure that you leave anyone from a Chinese culture with their dignity intact following discussions and negotiations. Losing face is a much bigger deal than it is in Western cultures. Be extra sensitive to their personal and cultural needs.

- It's business protocol in the Middle East to attend negotiations and deal-making discussions in sizeable delegations. If you don't do likewise they may feel that you don't attach as much importance to the discussions as they do.

The above just gives a thumbnail sketch of some of the dos and don'ts of connecting across continents. Each country and culture has its own rules and regulations, some written, some unwritten, and if you want to be a super-effective connector on the international stage you need to know them. In an increasingly global business world there is no doubt that cross-border trade will continue to bring people together. Your job as a connector is to come together harmoniously and effectively with your international counterparts – and that means avoiding the minefields of international protocol. Watch your step!

CHAPTER 8

Connecting Face to Face

MEETINGS ARE THE tried and tested way for people to pass
on information, solve problems, discuss issues, brain-
storm ideas, motivate others – and to sell themselves. They take
many forms, from formal boardroom-style deliberations
through small gatherings to one-on-one discussions. Whatever
guise it takes, there's no arguing with the fact that a face-to-face
meeting with one or more people puts you firmly in the spotlight – and to succeed you have to perform.

In this chapter we'll put each type of meeting under the
microscope and assess how you can squeeze the most out of
your involvement, whether you are a participant in a meeting or
leading it. We'll also cover how to really get your message across
when you are presenting your thoughts and ideas to a group.

Despite there being a vast difference in approach between a
14-member committee meeting and an informal chat over coffee, the connector's success factors are *exactly* the same. You will
be judged on:

- How prepared you are.

- What you say – and how you say it.

- How you behave.

- How well you listen.

And (would you believe it?):

- Where you sit!

We'll work down from the formality of big meetings to smaller discussions because the ground rules for big meetings form the bedrock of skills that the connector can adapt easily for smaller affairs.

While we all know instinctively what makes for a good meeting, the vast majority of get-togethers don't stick to the basic rules of timeliness and keeping to the point. The 'housekeeping' work of circulating information in advance (and expecting participants to have read the papers before the meeting) and producing clear minutes identifying who has agreed to do what and by when prepares the ground for a great meeting. There is nothing difficult in this. All that is required is good business discipline so that meetings are seen to be a platform for decision-making, not a 'talking shop' where no one around the table sees the value of having a meeting at all.

Successful Participation in Meetings

Rightly or wrongly, people will form impressions of you based on your performance at meetings and it is essential that you participate actively in the discussions. Studies have shown that at the start of a meeting participants' impressions of you are largely neutral if they have not met you before, but they will soon turn negative if you don't speak up or ask questions. So sitting still and keeping your mouth shut is actually harmful to your image!

At this point someone in the audience at my seminars will invariably raise their hand and say, 'I understand that point, but my problem is I don't know *what* to say – my comments somehow don't seem appropriate.' They often go on to say that they've seen that others seemingly have the gift of asking the right questions at the right time, 'chipping in' with well-timed observations and generally being seen as a much more valued member of the group. What's their secret? Luckily, it's not some God-given gift. In all likelihood they are following, whether they know it or not, the connector's six routes to contributing effectively to *any* meeting. Believe me, after working on these you'll be able to make a timely and relevant contribution too. So let's get down to it...

Prepare, prepare, prepare

This needs saying three times because if you do it properly it's your highway to making your contribution to the meeting. Neglect your preparation and you'll quickly find your ability to get involved hits a dead end. You've probably heard what my dad used to say to me – 'Proper preparation prevents pretty poor performance' – and he was right. Top connectors prepare properly because they know that this is the key to performing effectively, making an impact and being seen to know what they are talking about.

Mundane as it may seem, connectors make sure they have read the minutes of the last meeting (if there are any). They read the papers sent to them in advance and highlight anything which appears significant to them, they consider their position on the issues and they think about what questions they may ask. If there are any points they are unsure of, they'll make a note to seek clarification.

Reading the information may also have given them some ideas they may wish to test out in the meeting. All in all, where they can, connectors go into a meeting with a whole host of thoughts, ideas, questions and, above all, key points of information buzzing around in their head. They are ready to participate. Where connecting at meetings is concerned, ignorance is not bliss, it's the road to nowhere.

Know your facts

Not all meetings are called with the luxury of papers being circulated in advance, of course, but this doesn't take away the need for preparation. Indeed, if you know the subject for discussion (if you don't, why are you at the meeting in the first place?), the key question to ask yourself beforehand is an unusual one: 'What *don't* I know about this area?' This takes your thinking away from your preconceived ideas into areas such as 'What if I'm asked about...?' 'What would my response be on...?' 'How long would it take to...?' 'How much would it cost for...?'

You may find that you simply don't have enough knowledge to accurately answer some of the questions that may be raised, or you don't have enough facts at your fingertips to support your position on an issue. The solution, of course, is to go back and prepare. If you know your facts, the meeting participants will quickly see you as a reliable authority, not someone who has only brought their opinions with them.

There will be times, however, when facts just aren't available, particularly in subjective or emotive areas, which is great news for a connector who wants to participate in meetings – you'll have prepared as far as you can, but can quite legitimately check if others have any additional information, or simply ask a question which helps them to share their views.

Get there early

Would you like to choose the best seat at the table, have the opportunity to break the ice with some of the key players before the meeting and enjoy the chance to network with others? Then do what the best connectors do and get there early! At the very least it shows professionalism and interest that will be noticed, and it could bring you new opportunities even before the meeting gets under way.

Alternatively, you could disturb the meeting by apologetically arriving late and sneaking into the only seat left – usually the rickety one with the wobbly leg right in the corner. Then you have to try to get a flavour of what's going on before making your opening remark, hoping that someone hasn't already raised the same point.

Focus on the big issues

Big fish concentrate on big matters, and you should do the same. Leave the discussion of the minutiae to the little fish who, surprisingly often, will try to spend an inordinate amount of time on the not so important things.

All good meeting leaders know that the strategic issues are what need to be discussed, agreed and acted upon. So give your credibility – and promotion prospects – a boost by focusing your questions, observations and discussion points on these.

If you have something to say on the smaller details, do so, but avoid at all costs plunging to the depths of the discussion pool by squabbling over relatively unimportant 'scraps' with meeting participants. Such public behaviour is a surefire way of telling those in charge that you are not ready for higher things.

Make an early impact

The sooner you say something relevant, the higher your credibility. That's what the research says. It also says that the longer you leave it to join in the discussion, the more pressure you'll feel, the worse impression you'll make on your fellow participants and the less you'll enjoy the meeting. So the message couldn't be more crystal clear: get your (relevant) comment in early and the group will accept you more readily. You'll then have set yourself up for a participative and enjoyable session.

Asking questions is the key to credibility

Watch the professional interviewers on the news, the newscasters who interview politicians, business leaders, trade unionists and others who have public accountability when things have gone wrong or there's a contentious issue to debate. How much time to do you think they have to research an issue in the depth they need to ask probing questions of the high-profile interviewees? Often only hours, sometimes very much less. But consider how they control the discussion through timely and relevant questions, questions that make interviewees think and viewers say, 'I would have asked that one.'

That's exactly the top connector's mindset and preparation for meetings. Just like the UK's journalist anchorman Jeremy Paxman or the States' Walter Kronkite they *prepare* by gathering information on the subject and the issues, they make absolutely sure of their *facts* and they focus entirely on the *big issues*. No messing about with irrelevancies for them – they want to know what the present situation is, how it will affect people, what is being done about it and what will happen next. And they do all of this, of course, by *making statements of fact and asking questions*. Do the same in your meetings.

Address your comments to the chairman

It is accepted protocol in formal meetings to address your comments to the chairman, not to other members of the group. The reason is obvious – if you are not careful the meeting degenerates into a series of sub-discussions with people talking across each other, often on different subjects. Experienced meeting-goers will no doubt have seen this syndrome. It's not always the fault of a bad chairman, but it is definitely the result of bad manners on the part of the offending participants. If you want to be seen as a top connector, don't indulge. Instead, help the chairman keep the meeting in order.

Use other people's comments as a bridge to yours

Rather than blurt out your comments and hope that you get your say in at the right time, the elegant way to do it is to use the comments of the person speaking as a link to yours. For example:

'I understand Kate's point and agree with what she says about ... I can also see ...' then make your comment.
'I agree with Harry and would add ...'
'Coming back to Jane's earlier thought on ..., I see it like this ...'

In this way you show that you recognise other people's contribution (whether you agree with it or not) and that you have been listening to what they say.

Get to the point

'Short and sharp' is the key phrase here. We've all sat in meetings where someone has pontificated on some point or other and clearly bored half the meeting to the edge of sleep while angering the other half.

Connectors know that the best way to make a point is to concentrate on the essentials, keep the message clear and use 'sound bites' just as the politicians do. Why? Because most people's attention span is short and the best way to capture it is to keep a message short, pithy and relevant. Think how much information a TV reporter gets across in a 90-second report. If they can do it, so can you. Watch them, adapt their style for your next meeting and see the impact you make... You'll be surprised!

Be interested

You can only connect fully in a meeting if you are interested in what's going on – and that means listening to others' opinions and evaluating them. Who knows, they may help you to change your preconceived ideas! It also means following the discussion, not just waiting for your pet subject to come up. Connectors treat meetings as a learning experience. They watch people's body language (fascinating in itself), attempt to distinguish fact from opinion and are constantly on the lookout for opportunities – new ideas, fresh ways of doing things, new contacts and information that will be valuable. Formal meetings need never be dull and boring again if you adopt the connector's mindset.

IN PRACTICE

ASDA, the UK retailing giant part of the US-based Wal-Mart retail empire, embodies the principles of having super-productive meetings in half the time. They do it by having no chairs in the meeting rooms!

Seriously, they have waist-high 'tables' where meeting attendees stand to discuss the issues on the agenda. The physical act of standing creates the urgency and focus required to get to the point and concentrate on the matters at hand. There's no leaning back on chairs, hands behind head, pontificating. There's no ceremonial pouring of tea. Instead you get a dynamic meeting of equals, sharp discussion and quick decisions. It's a tremendous approach.

The Connector's Way to Chair a Meeting

The connector really needs to show their mettle when they are responsible for chairing a meeting. A great performance will reflect on their abilities, as will a bad one. But what are the ingredients of a successful meeting?

There really is no secret to the basics and experienced connectors know that getting the fundamentals right sets the scene for a meeting that really produces results. But too many of us forget them in the hurly burly of our daily schedules. So, let's recap on the 'connector's checklist' for running formal meetings. Connectors:

Make sure there's an agenda circulated in advance, covering:

- The objectives of the meeting.

- The points to be covered and, where appropriate, the discussion time allocated to each.

- The start and finish times and location of the meeting.

Protect their time and ask, from a personal perspective, these five questions:

1. What is the point of the meeting?

2. Why am I attending?

3. What can I contribute?

4. Am I the best/right person to go?

5. How can I get the most out of it and use my time effectively?

Get the right people there

The ace connector's aim is always to have the minimum number of the *right* people present at a meeting. While cutting down numbers is not always easy due to the politics concerned, connectors usually know from bitter experience that meetings of more than 10 rarely achieve the pace and results they are seeking. Four or five relevant people can often achieve a good deal more.

For connectors operating in an organisation that has big meetings, one way to encourage smaller numbers is to invite only the essential players, but to send a note to all the other interested parties with the agenda stating that they are welcome to attend *if* they have something specific to contribute. This approach weeds out those who would have attended just to be seen to be involved.

The connector then completes the circle of communication by sending the action points from the meeting to all those individuals originally circulated the agenda. In this way they won't feel isolated and will be kept fully in the picture on important decisions.

Up the tempo

Everyone has a responsibility to keep the meeting moving. When you are chairing, make it a policy to start on time and emphasise this fact politely to latecomers – they won't do it again. Don't waste participants' time either – stamp on anything trivial and move it 'outside the meeting'. Many a meeting is hijacked by one individual who insists on monopolising the discussion and they get away with it simply because the other attendees allow them to. On the other hand, be flexible on timing if real progress on a 'meaty' issue is being made.

Urgency concentrates the mind. A meeting scheduled an hour before lunch or late in the afternoon can be rattled through because participants' mindsets are right – they recognise that they have limited time for discussion and getting to the point is easier.

Never allow interruptions to the meeting unless absolutely necessary. The momentum can quickly evaporate if participants leave to answer mobile phones or deal with messages being passed through by secretaries.

To keep the momentum, if you have to eat, do it while you are discussing, but make sure you do allow time for a laugh and a joke – there's no substitute for face-to-face interaction to build relationships and nobody said meetings have to be dull, boring affairs!

Capture decisions

Meetings are usually called to make decisions. So make sure any commitments made are clear and that participants go away knowing precisely what to do. Talk without constructive follow-up action is usually wasted time.

Get people involved – and committed

Top connectors within organisations recognise that getting people together regularly (for example weekly) as a team can be very time-efficient, particularly if they have a rule where people save up their non-urgent problems for the meeting. It clears their diary, which can often be blocked by such time-absorbing discussions during the rest of the week.

Weekly meetings are also superb for keeping your people 'on vision', whatever your goals may be. Simply ask them to address these two questions:

- What *have I done* to help us move closer to our goals?

- What *am I going to do* this week to move us closer to our goals?

In no time at all you'll have your team members thinking on the Wednesday before your Friday meeting: 'What can I say this week? What *have* I done to help us move closer to our goals?' You wouldn't get anywhere near the same level of ownership of the vision if you didn't regularly ask the questions.

At the end of your meetings do a quick 'round table' update on opportunities and issues. People may agree to do things that would not have surfaced otherwise. Make sure these actions are captured in the minutes. And make sure that whoever is capturing the action points for the meeting circulates them as quickly as possible – the same day is by far the best, for it shows urgency and the importance you attach to the actions. Ensure that the action points cover who has committed to do what and by when. There's no need for a full regurgitation of the discussion, just concentrate on the actions.

Focus on speedy action

Top connector chairmen challenge people rigorously if they haven't done the things they committed to doing by the due date (and that's another reason to get the action points out quickly). They know that otherwise they will constantly be dealing with excuses and covering old ground and their meetings will be in danger of falling into the 'nothing ever happens' category. So they encourage peer pressure to complete your agreed actions by the meeting.

These simple keys to connecting effectively in meetings will ensure that participants come charged up for a powerful and productive session.

TRY THIS

Critically review the meetings you attend. How could they be improved? Then ask yourself the most important question of all: do you really need the meeting and, if so, do *you* have to be there?

If it's appropriate, why not issue a one-pager with your own ground rules for meetings? It's one way to reinforce the message to your people that you want short, pithy, action-oriented meetings. Poor meetings cost you money; good ones can create a platform for making it.

If you can't get face to face, try videoconferencing or telephone conference calls with a time limit. It's often amazing how much you can get through if everyone is prepared and plays the game by the 'good meeting' ground rules.

'How Was It for You?'

Think of a meeting that you recently attended or chaired, and answer the following questions as honestly as you can. Then consider the implications of your answers for your own networking effectiveness on that occasion.

The Dynamics of a Meeting	Yes	No
1. Was the outcome worth the time you spent in the meeting?	☐	☐
2. Did you have a clear understanding of what contribution you were expected to make?	☐	☐
3. Did you make that contribution?	☐	☐
4. Did you receive an agenda before the meeting?	☐	☐
5. Were you able to contribute to it?	☐	☐
6. Were relevant background papers circulated before the meeting?	☐	☐

7. Did you have enough time to read them? ☐ ☐

8. Did you know the other participants in the meeting and their roles? ☐ ☐

9. Did you (or others) introduce yourselves? ☐ ☐

10. Did the meeting start on time? ☐ ☐

11. Was a finish time set? ☐ ☐

12. Did you stick to it? ☐ ☐

13. Was the meeting too long? ☐ ☐

14. Did you speak as much as you would have wanted? ☐ ☐

15. Did you feel that you listened effectively? ☐ ☐

16. Did you ask questions of the participants? ☐ ☐

17. Was someone responsible for taking notes of the actions agreed? ☐ ☐

18. Was a personal responsibility and a deadline given for each action? ☐ ☐

19. Have you received a copy of the actions yet? ☐ ☐

20. Have you done your actions yet?! ☐ ☐

Smaller Gatherings

So much for larger meetings, but what about those small, often informal gatherings? How you perform in these situations is just as essential to your success as a connector. Whether it's a one-on-one sales discussion or you are trying to persuade a small group of the benefits of your approach, it's critical to look at the situation from your contact's point of view.

The contact's perspective

Your contact's decision on whom they want to work with will very often be forged in the face-to-face time they spend with you. Their selection is mostly intuitive, personal and based on that impression of you. How you behave in meetings with them will be seen as a very real indication of how you would perform 'on the job'.

There are many clues your contact might look for to assess the kind of person you are and whether they want to form a business relationship with you. David Maister, the undisputed master of Professional Services Marketing, captured the buyer's attitude magnificently when he penned these (slightly adapted) 14 'perspectives':

1. The first thing that will catch my attention is your preparation. Being unprepared not only reveals laziness, but also that you don't have a special interest in me and my perspective.

2. Preparation is also your opportunity to demonstrate initiative. I will be a lot more impressed with something that has been put together especially for me as opposed to your pre-printed brochure.

3. I do not want to hear about you; I want to talk about me and my situation. I hate to be sold to, but I may be willing to buy.

4. First you must make me feel comfortable. Perhaps ask me what's going well. Give me some *new* information. Tell me what you've been doing for other organisations like mine. Find a way to help.

5. Give me an education. Tell me about alternate ways of dealing with the common problems of my industry. Ask me how I am doing things now and use that as an opportunity to help me understand some options I may have for doing things differently. Don't be afraid to float high-risk ideas early ('just an idea').

6. I won't believe your claims about your expertise until you give me some evidence to back them up. For example, don't tell me about your experience in my industry (or on a particular topic), but ask questions that reveal your knowledge.

7. Don't patronise me by trying to tell me what's going on in my business. Don't say: 'These are the three most important things going on in your industry' but 'Our experience suggests that these are the three most important things. Do you agree?' Turn your assertions into questions.

8. Your manner of speech, how you choose to phrase your sentences, tells me something about how you deal with clients. Make our meeting a conversation. Don't talk all the time and similarly don't grill me.

9. Show an understanding of my role – who my boss is, how I'm measured, what my budgets are. Then I'll believe you are treating me as a person, not a corporate entity.

10. Don't start telling me how you can solve my problems until I have acknowledged my problems, needs, wants and concerns. Ask good questions and listen.

11. Show your sensitivity. For instance, asking: 'What don't you have time for?' will go down much better than: 'What are your problems?'

12. If I do begin to show interest in a given issue, your next task is to convince me (or get me to convince myself) that the issue is big enough to bother with. Help me picture the benefits you can bring and then I'll take an interest in what else you have to say.

13. Don't rush to give me a singular, concrete answer concerning 'your approach' – give me options. By letting me choose, I can see you are the type of person who will respect my judgement and involve me.

14. Give me reasons and reasoning I can use when I consult with my superiors and colleagues. Make your objective for the meeting one of making progress in our relationship.

How the Experts Do It

Basic as it sounds, experienced connectors know the value of getting the fundamentals right. How are you going to get to the meeting, what will you wear, where will you sit (if it is possible to influence it) in relation to your contact(s)?

Top connectors ease smoothly into the meeting by:

- Effectively managing their greetings and introductions.

- Using small talk to get settled in, then setting the scene by telling their contact what they want to get out of the meeting and asking for their objectives and the points they would wish to discuss.

- Checking how much time their contact has available and that the agenda meets with their approval.

- Explaining the role of anyone they have brought with them to the meeting.

They share their knowledge and understanding of a situation and provide their own insight by:

- Describing the relevant issue, idea or opportunity.

- Highlighting why they think it may be important to their contact.

They test their ideas, watching the contact's reactions carefully. By asking questions they can identify areas where they are off-beam, home in on areas of agreement and keep focused.

They ask strategic and engaging questions that generate interest and focus attention on their contact's critical issues. Such questions show that the connector understands their contact's business, or is at least seeking to.

A good discussion in a meeting will almost certainly lead to the identification (on both sides) of areas for further exploration or agreed solutions to problems. Equally importantly the connector will get a solid 'feel' for what is really important and how they can help.

Inevitably, in discussions of this kind, when the connector is testing their ideas and presenting potential ways forward, they will come across objections. Great news! Top connectors have trained themselves to welcome objections, not dread them. They know that an objection helps guide them to what their contact feels is important and relevant.

IN PRACTICE

The Top Connectors' Creed

The hallmarks of top connectors during a face-to-face contact are:

1. They explicitly state their understanding of the objectives for the contact and invite others to do the same.

2. They keep in line with the objectives of the contact and do not wander off down irrelevant sidetracks. If one approach is not working, they have the flexibility to continually adjust their style.

3. They explain themselves and seek clarification from others where needed.

4. They keep their verbal and non-verbal behaviour in step with one another.

5. They conduct themselves in such a way that you believe them to be genuine and are not suspicious of ulterior motives.

6. They behave in such a way that you feel at ease and satisfied, for example they use your name, look at you sufficiently, show that they have heard what you said and support or build on your ideas more often than they reject them.

7. They never acquiesce silently (because they know that silence is infuriatingly difficult for others to interpret).

8. They produce explicit suggestions and proposals that contain a

possible course of action rather than an implied one. They push for the agreement of specific action plans rather than being content with intentions.

9. They never get into a disagreement spiral. When wrong or inadequate in some way, they admit it rather than pretend that they are right.

10. When criticising someone they are always constructive, in the sense that they produce a suggestion along with every criticism.

How to Lose Friends and Influence in Meetings – Quickly

The six cardinal sins to avoid in meetings are:

1. Talking more than listening, which means that you discover less about your contact and their needs and priorities. Overdone, you also come across as dominating, and even manipulative.

2. Using 'red rag' words and phrases that irritate and antagonise, for example 'with due respect …', 'I hear what you say, but …', 'obviously…'

3. Making counter-proposals. If you don't like what others are saying, ask questions to help them think it through rather than coming up with a suggestion of your own. If someone's proposal triggers a good idea in your mind, don't just blurt it out.

4. Stacking up arguments to support your proposition. Rather than making a stronger case, it sounds as though you're making excuses. If you have to give that many reasons to bolster your case, it must be a poor one.

5. Persistently using the royal 'we' – it comes over as being weak or lacking the courage of your convictions. Hiding behind the corporate 'we' often means you do not want to do something.

6. Using 'formal speak' and jargon. At best it creates distance from others in the meeting, but worse than that, they may not even understand what you are on about!

The Psychology of Seating Positions

As shown in the diagram below, where you sit in a meeting depends on what you are trying to achieve. If you are a participant, it is best to sit directly opposite the chairman if you want major involvement in the proceedings. Why? Because you can much more easily catch the chairman's eye in order to ask a question or make a comment. Think of an auctioneer who can spot the body language of a bidder from the most subtle of gestures. It's the same in meetings. You can signal to an astute chairman that you want to make a contribution without actually saying a word. But it's difficult to do so if you are sitting right next to the chairman. In this position it is hard

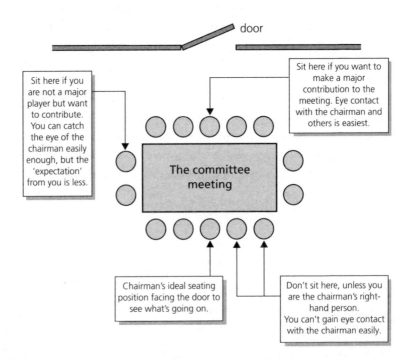

door

Sit here if you want to make a major contribution to the meeting. Eye contact with the chairman and others is easiest.

Sit here if you are not a major player but want to contribute. You can catch the eye of the chairman easily enough, but the 'expectation' from you is less.

The committee meeting

Chairman's ideal seating position facing the door to see what's going on.

Don't sit here, unless you are the chairman's right-hand person.
You can't gain eye contact with the chairman easily.

to use your body language and eye contact effectively – you literally have to 'speak up' in order to achieve the result.

If there are other players who are recognised as more important in the meeting, try to sit at a 45-degree angle to the chairman. This keeps you in their peripheral vision and therefore seen, but not in the prime eye contact location where your contribution is 'expected'.

Sitting on the same side as the chairman, especially if there are a number of people in the meeting, is counter-productive to your aims because they will not be able to see you!

The Secrets of Successful Presentations

Organisations can sometimes spend thousands of pounds, and sometimes years, in getting the opportunity to present, face to face, to key contacts at a potential client. On the personal level, for many people in organisations, contractors or consultants, the highest test of their career is to present to the board their thoughts on what needs to be done. The ability to connect with those whose decision can have a sometimes life-changing effect on your future can't be understated. But why do some people succeed while others fail miserably?

There's a lot of truth in the old adage 'It's not what you say, it's the way you say it' and this is particularly so when presenting. Even the most interesting topic can be rendered dull and lifeless by a poor delivery, but the reverse is also the case. The driest of technical subjects can be made to sparkle if the presenter makes it relevant to the audience and maintains their interest through variety in presentation style, voice, pitch, gesture, visual aids, and so on. That's what the connectors who win at presentations do and I'll share their methods with you here.

'Do you always do this?'

Whether it's an informal discussion or one with the backing of a full audio-visual production, the successful presenter *always* does this: they ask themselves 'What *is* my message?' and 'How best can I convey it?' These are simple but profound questions, and most presentation failures can be traced to not fully addressing them.

Connectors know that their message *must* be memorable and thought-provoking. It must be pitched at the level of those listening, use the words they would use and be delivered at a pace of speech they will be comfortable with. Good presenters know that their body language will say as much as the words they utter and they recognise that appropriate showmanship sets them apart from the 'also rans'.

No matter what the subject, there are certain things that your audience – the board of directors, the purchasing team or your entire organisation's employees – will want. Deliver them and your success is almost assured. What do they want?

They want to be:

- Impressed.

- Convinced.

- Reassured.

- Informed.

They also want to know:

- What the benefits of your ideas are.

- What they will cost.

- The results they can expect.

- When they can expect them.

That's the blueprint for any connector's presentation, and the champs make theirs really come to life. Here's how you can do the same.

Soothe your nerves by planning ahead

Everyone has nerves before an important presentation. But nerves, if not controlled, can ruin your delivery and spoil all your previous hard work. Luckily, there are lots of things you can do to reduce their effects. Consider these:

- Research your audience in advance and script your presentation accordingly. What do they really want to hear?

- Rehearse until you are familiar with your key points.

- Consider what you will do if things don't go to plan. Having a fall-back plan helps you to relax.

- Tell yourself that your audience wants your presentation to succeed. They do – no one wants to listen to a nervous or boring presenter!

Get them on your side

You are not going to persuade your contact, or anyone on the decision-making team, if you don't impress them. Luckily, many of the actions you need to take to get the potential client on your side are basic – and that's exactly the reason why many presenters forget them. Think back to the last time you spoke to a group and compare your approach against these 'best practice' tips:

- Note the seating position of the members of the group; it can reveal a lot about the hierarchy. Act accordingly.

- Dress to mirror your potential client's style.

- Respect their territory – don't move the furniture without their permission.

- Acknowledge your potential client (and other members of the team) by name and thank them for their time.

- Tell them how long your presentation will take and stick to it.

- Use a speaking style that is relevant to them. Are they quick thinkers, analysers or other character types?

- Don't make claims without facts to back you up. Use proof statements, examples and case studies to bolster your credibility.

- Most important of all, show enthusiasm. Enthusiasm is the single most important thing in a presentation. Show them that you believe in your ideas. If your presentation says nothing else, you will still beat any grey-faced opposition.

Come from their perspective

When presenting to the people who can make a decision about your ideas, it's critical to see the issue as they see it. Don't waste your time trying to change the beliefs of your audience; instead, show how your ideas reinforce their attitudes.

How do you know what their beliefs and attitudes are? Try these approaches:

- Develop an audience profile by researching the likely different levels of understanding of your message and what people's objections and questions will probably be.

- Identify the sub-groups within the decision-making group and make sure that you understand and meet their different needs. For example, a chief executive is likely to have a different perception from the marketing, finance or IT director. What are the differences and how can you address them?

- Predict the selling points your competitors will make and minimise them by making your own counterpoints.

Detect the decision-maker

Someone needs to say 'yes' to you and your ideas, and it's important to know who that person is. Too often presenters have focused on influencing the wrong person, someone who is not the ultimate decision-maker. Take a tip from the champion presenters and:

- Identify where the person who holds the purse strings is sitting.

- Make sure you cover what *they* want to hear.

- Influence them by showing due deference, address them by name and show that you respect their power by looking at them more than the others. Why would they choose you if you have 'slighted' them by not recognising their power or specific needs?

Build rapid rapport

You can't be a good presenter without creating rapport. Without it you can't develop the warmth you are seeking between yourself and your audience. There are some practical actions you can build into your repertoire in order to get that rapport going quickly:

- Maintain a gentle, non-confrontational eye contact. Look at your audience's shoulders or ears – it is a less challenging contact than eye to eye, but still appears personal.

- Switch your eye contact continually between the group members.

- Address individuals periodically by name, where appropriate.

- Smile and demonstrate enthusiasm – it's infectious!

- Use pauses and changes of pace to add texture to your presentation.

- Use your body language to best effect. Slow, open gestures with palms towards the audience are positive; avoid brisk, jabbing gestures, closed fists or chopping motions. Research has shown that these tend to make your audience irritated or angry.

- If you have to, use small cue cards rather than a script. A script makes it difficult to maintain eye contact and build rapport and tends to indicate that you don't know your stuff ... even when you do!

Tailored, not 'off the peg'

An 'off-the-peg' standard presentation which contains generic messages intended for any client anywhere is not going to help you to win business. Just as the high-class tailor takes great pains to measure every conceivable distance and angle when fitting someone for a 'tailor-made' suit, so the connector tailors their material, asking: 'How does what I'm saying relate *specifically* to my audience?' If it doesn't, the connector will either make it relevant or leave it out.

Create a compelling script

Facts alone aren't enough to persuade. You need to generate emotion in your audience, to paint a picture of the benefits you're offering and to get them to take some positive action. Keep your message short, snappy and credible:

- Be clear about what you want to change in the audience's attitude or present situation.

- Add credibility to your opening remarks by explaining why you are qualified to make the presentation.

- Your audience will have a short attention span (20 minutes maximum), so structure your script accordingly. Keep it punchy and packed with key messages.

Provide 'signposts'

Your audience needs some 'signposts' to help them get a feel for the material you are about to cover and to understand why it is important to them. While this seems to be encouraging the speaker to go over the same ground again, in practice this is not the case. 'Tell them what you are going to tell them, tell them, and tell them what you've told them' is good advice for any presenter.

The introduction may only last a minute, but in that time the top presenter will have told the audience why the subject is important, why they should listen, what areas will be covered and how the material will be presented.

In the bulk of the presentation the connector will elaborate on these points and highlight key issues relevant to the audience.

In the final summing up (again this may only be a couple of minutes) the connector will bring it all together by recapping on the key message and explaining any actions the audience needs to take. It's a logical, easy and structured way to deliver a quality presentation.

'The evidence is clear, your honour'

We have all sat through enough court-room dramas on television to know that what convinces the jury is evidence – hard, compelling evidence. It's the same in presentations. While the greatest talker in the world can convince up to a point, the 'jury' (in the case, the decision-making panel) will want proof. That's why the connector uses case studies of what has been successful before, references from relevant clients, demonstrations of how it will work, mock-ups, diagrams and anything else which says: 'This is evidence to show that I can deliver what I promise.'

Involve the audience

A 'talking head', someone who just stands up and presents, is easy to listen to for five minutes, harder for ten and can be downright boring after twenty! While the presenter's skills are obviously important in keeping interest levels high, the longer they go on, the more they are fighting an attribute of the human condition: attention span.

As the pace of the business life gets faster, people become

impatient far more quickly (ever get upset because your computer isn't processing quickly enough or you are stuck in slow-moving traffic?) So it is with presentations. The audience's minds can quickly wander. And the connector knows that they need to keep them right there – not by talking, but by involving them. Asking rhetorical questions is one way; getting them involved in a demonstration or a discussion is another.

Assume the business

A common dilemma for connectors in tender presentations is whether or not to assume winning the work. It is the difference between saying 'If we win the business we will…' and 'When we meet you on a monthly basis, we will…'

'If' has the psychological effect of reinforcing any doubt in the decision-maker's mind, so think positively and talk as if the work has already been given to you. Then you'll naturally talk about 'when' rather than 'if'.

Using visual aids

The decision whether or not to use visual aids is an individual one and depends largely on the material to be presented, the expectations of the potential client and even the dimensions of the room itself. If you do decide to use visual aids there are a number of options, each with their advantages and disadvantages (*see below*). The key points to bear in mind for successful use of visual aids are:

- Bring your own equipment – on the day you don't want the shock of finding that the equipment provided does not work or is incompatible with your requirements.

- Make your visuals dynamic … and readable.

- Put your potential client's name on them – it tailors the presentation and shows that you have taken time to consider their needs.

- Lay out the room so that your visuals can be seen. This is critical! There is nothing worse than arriving to present your material and having to move the entire equipment or audience to make sure that they can see your visuals. It's unprofessional and gets you off to a bad start, so make sure that you research the room first.

- Don't let your visuals dominate. They should support your key messages, not be a poor substitute for them.

Choose the right horse for the right course

Any visual aid you use will have an effect on the type of presentation you give, the atmosphere you create in the room and how your message is received. There is no right and wrong answer, but don't just go at it blindly. Think about what you are trying to achieve, and in what environment, and act accordingly.

- **Computer graphics projector** Advantages: quick and easy to produce quality visuals and project them direct from your computer. Looks very professional and high tech. Disadvantages: needs time (and expertise) to set up. Needs space to project onto a wall or screen. Possibility of major disaster if the computer fails in some way!

- **Overhead projector** Advantages: very familiar, everyone can use one. Can be used in a limited space, inexpensive to produce slides. Disadvantages: transparencies are not as professional as computer graphics.

- **Flipcharts** Advantages: can be used in a small space. Give a 'hands-on' feel to your presentation. Disadvantages: you need to able to write clearly, spell properly and know what you want to say in advance. Difficult to maintain presentation flow and eye contact while writing.

- **Desktop presenters** Advantages: easy to prepare; useful low-tech visual devices for very small audiences. Disadvantages: no use for any more than two or three people. Can be perceived as a 'salesman's tool' by the potential client.

- **'Talking' book** Advantages: easily produced, low-tech visual device which gives structure to your presentation. Disadvantages: the audience tends to read the book or flip forward rather than listen to what you say.

Each visual device has its merits and its place – the choice is yours. You may choose to use no visual aids at all, or one which suits the recipient. The main point to bear in mind is that any visuals you use should be of the highest quality and reflect the standards you intend to provide. Anything less will detract from your presentation.

THE CONNECTOR'S TOOLKIT

Using visual aids

Do

- Save your computer-based presentation on a spare disk as a back up. We all know what happens with technology at the worst possible moment!

- Stand away from the visual aid as you talk.

- Give attendees time to read and digest what's on the screen (another good reason for not putting too much onto a slide).

- Test the equipment in plenty of time and practise with it so that you can move from one visual aid to another confidently and effortlessly.

- Use a pointer if you need to refer to particular images (or figures) on your slide.

- Turn off the projector if you are speaking for some time without the use of a visual aid, or use a 'blank' slide with a colour that's restful on the eye.

- Practise 'handovers' with the previous and following speakers. Weak handovers show lack of preparation and look unprofessional.

- Check your slides for any typing errors or incorrect figures. People do spot them and lose concentration and in turn you lose credibility.

Don't

- Turn your back on the audience to refer to your visual aids. You can glance at your aid by all means, but do face the audience for the vast majority of the time.

- Stand in front of the screen. Have consideration too for people at the side of the seminar room. You may be blocking their view.

- Give out handouts unless you want your audience to read them while you are presenting.

- Rely on anyone else to check that your slides are in the right order or that the equipment works. It's you who will be in the spotlight if anything goes wrong, so be responsible for doing your own checks.

- Unnecessarily brandish a pointer – it distracts the audience.

- Read the words of the slide as part of your presentation – it bores the audience (they can all read). Instead, paraphrase, shorten and summarise the points, or draw attention to the key message. Get some life into it!

- Have too many slides. Each one must be of value in its own right, not just a poor prop for you to remember what you want to say.

Delivering a powerful close

We easily forget information given to us (if you don't believe it, try to recall now what you read two pages ago – chances are that you can't). The best presenters know that it is crucial to encapsulate their key messages in a powerful closing statement, simply to make sure that their audience remembers them. At this stage it's important to:

- Regain the audience's attention. A long presentation has a tendency to lose people if you're not careful.

- Return to your opening theme.

- Summarise your key ideas – five at most, ideally no more than three.

- Re-establish your credibility to do the work.

- Paint a picture of the advantages and future benefits of taking you on.

- Get some *emotion* in there, and thank your audience, genuinely, for their time.

Detecting the silent messages

We've already seen the power of body language in rapport-building. The ace connector knows how to read the non-verbal signs of an audience which say 'Go on' or 'I'm not convinced', 'I'm bored' or, worst of all, 'You've no chance.'

Be alert to body language that *may* give away the thoughts and views of your audience. Here are some moves to look out for while you are presenting. What if your audience, in particular your key decision-maker, is:

- **Leaning backwards, losing eye contact and reading papers** You're in danger of losing them or you've said something they don't agree with. Top connectors will change tack here by asking a question or involving their audience. The key is to halt a potential downward spiral and re-engage.

- **Folding their arms** It could mean that they are cold, uncomfortable with what you have just said or simply aren't yet willing to be on your side. Connectors know that this could be a signal for proof of their point or a 'bugle call' to get the decision-maker involved by asking them to do something physical – read a brochure, turn a page in the handout, come up to the flipchart, and so on.

■ **Leaning towards you with upright posture** You've no need for me to tell you that this is someone who is eager to hear what you have to say, or at least is open to be persuaded. You instinctively recognise the 'I'm interested' message – which is great news for you. That's not to say your job is done. 'Interested' doesn't mean 'convinced' – and convinced is what brings you success.

Don't forget your own body language

You've seen the immense importance of appropriate eye contact and open gestures, and how critical the seating plan is in creating the right atmosphere in the room (*see page 192*).

Ace connectors also borrow from the magician's toolkit to direct their audience's attention. Just as a magic wand is a superb instrument for attracting people's gaze, so is a pointer or even a pen for a presenter. Pointing at a visual aid or a specific item in a report or presentation material is a great way to gain – or regain – your audience's focus. Try it!

Presentations can often be the pinnacle of a connector's work with contacts. The skills are the same whether it is a job interview, a presentation to a committee, the board of your company or a 'pitch' for a new assignment. Being prepared and understanding your audience's perspective are the twin keys to a dazzling presentation.

CHAPTER 9

Connecting on the Phone

WE'VE PROBABLY ALL been in a position where we've taken a call from a person whose voice is like pure silk and whose tone is immediately attractive. During your conversation you'll have formed a favourable picture of the owner of the voice and the personality that goes with it. That's the impact of a great connector on the telephone.

Connectors know that they have to use all the attributes at their disposal to come over well on the phone. In face-to-face situations a large proportion of a person's impression of you is your appearance and body language. This, of course, changes dramatically when you're on the phone. Now your contact has nothing more to go on than the pace, pitch and tone of your voice. So how do you make it really create that 'favourable picture' of you?

Building Phone Rapport

When you're on the phone, your voice tells the whole story, so you have to get some fizz into it! After all, it's the only clue you can give to your listener about your personality. You may be gesticulating wildly and using great body language, but this will be of little consequence to the person on the other end of the line. However, don't lose the gestures – using them as you would do normally greatly helps to create a natural pace and flow to your conversation, and your voice will sound more relaxed, natural and friendly as a result.

On the phone you'll need to put more of your silent body language 'energy' into your voice by giving verbal rather than non-verbal signs. I'm talking here about using encouraging lines like 'Go on' and 'Tell me more', and sympathisers like 'I can imagine how you feel' and 'I understand'. These demonstrate your interest in what your telephone conversation partner is saying and show that you are genuinely listening. In particular, use your contact's name more often than you would in a face-to-face encounter – it keeps their attention!

At one time or another we've all had the quiet listener who gave no verbal cues and we have stopped what we were saying to ask: 'Are you still there?' This type of telephone contact is unnerving because you're not sure whether the other person is interested or not, annoyed by what you are saying or OK about it. Overall the 'silent treatment' is very hard to deal with, so don't be the perpetrator of it. Instead give plenty of verbal encouragement to your phone partner and stay actively involved with the call.

Become an Information Detective

For many connectors in business, the phone is likely to be the source of most conversations with contacts, and it's those very conversations which can provide you with a vast treasure of information that will help you to build rapport and friendships – if you take the time to identify and store it.

We've covered this already, so there's no need to labour the point, but gathering information on your contacts' likes and dislikes, issues of the day and the longer-term and personal stuff like family, hobbies, sports and interests is the starting-point for strong bonds.

The elegant way for a connector to do this is to have a contact card (a Rolodex file will do) or even a hard-backed A5 or A4 pad to capture key items of information as they arise in conversation.

Nobody wants to be interrogated about their personal situation and business issues, of course, so be sensible and let these come out naturally as you begin to build a relationship (each will need to run at its own pace), with the occasional prompt from you. A question such as 'What's happening at your place?' can lead to a discussion on current business and workplace issues for your contact and 'What did you get up to at the weekend?' might reveal a wonderland of hobbies, interests, likes and dislikes. The important thing here is not to pry, but to capture the information that is freely given.

As your relationship develops, you can introduce some of the knowledge you have gained back into your later discussions, for instance by asking how your contact managed to sort out the production problem they were having last time you spoke, how that big golf game at the weekend went, if the family enjoyed their holiday break on the coast, and so on. It shows that you had been listening and that you are interested.

Just a quick word of warning at this point: don't play back *everything* your contact has told you – there's a fine social line between interest and overinterest. Each contact's 'line' will be different, so be sensitive.

'Kiss' the Call

'Keep it short and sweet' (kiss) is the connector's watchword here. Rambling is for country holidays, not the telephone. On the phone it is vital that you get to the point quickly so, after introducing yourself, get straight into the purpose of the call. Frame it from your contact's perspective: what's in it for them, what do they need to know and why, what do you want them to do ... and why should they do it?

Not all phone conversations you have will be in 'sales' mode, but nevertheless thinking through the benefit of your call to your contact is a discipline well worth cultivating. It will help you to have more focused conversations and leave your contact with the feeling that time spent on the phone with you is both pleasant and helpful.

Take a tip from the sales professionals here: never leave the scene of a phone call without an agreement on the next action. The action may well be to do nothing for the time being, but at least you'll have both agreed that this is the right move.

Alternatively, the agreement could simply be that you'll call again in a couple of weeks or that you'll check out the availability of a golf tee time for you both – whatever it is, large or small, capture it there and then, otherwise it's in danger of being forgotten. And what may appear insignificant to you may not be treated the same way by your phone contact. So, if you forget to call again in two weeks as promised or the tee time check goes completely out of your mind, don't be surprised if you get a cooler reception next time you speak to that person. Your credibility will have taken a dent and your contact's confidence in you will have diminished. The connector's approach is to capture the actions, large or small, *and do them*.

Adapting the Professional Seller's Phone Secrets

All of what's been said so far about keeping conversations short and punchy, ramping up your phone 'personality' through voice and verbal 'encouragers', using your contact's name and capturing nuggets of relevant information are meat and drink to the professional who uses the phone to develop relationships. Here are some more specific tips from the professionals.

Getting past the PA

Over the years, such champion connectors have learned to cold call heavy hitters who are normally protected by their Personal

Assistant (PA) early in the morning before normal business starts or at close of play when the majority of other workers have left for the evening. These can be the best times to land the big fish who will answer their own phone if there's no one else there to do it.

'Is this a good time?'

The connector will also check with the contact whether it is a convenient time to talk. You can't see the chaos and panic at the other end of the phone because that report needs to be out of the door in five minutes but, clearly, trying to persuade your contact of the value of your idea or product at such a time is fruitless. Not only will they have their mind on other matters, but you'll also have left the possibly indelible impression that you are the nuisance who hindered them at the crucial moment. So be professional and check whether it is convenient to speak by saying 'Are you OK to talk just now?' or 'Do you have a couple of minutes to talk?'

If the answer is 'no', do what the pros do and agree a time to talk. In effect, you've created a telephone 'appointment' which most contacts will keep. When you do get to speak you'll generally find your contact grateful for your earlier help and in a much better frame of mind to hear what you have to say.

'Great, it's a date'

Once you've made your 'pitch', if it's an appointment you're after, increase your chances of getting it by using the connector's approach to the 'alternative close'. It's worked for years and goes like this: when seeking an appointment, keep control of the situation by proposing a date *and* an alternative so that your contact can't easily refuse. For example: 'How about 3 p.m. next Wednesday, or 4 p.m. on Thursday perhaps?' If the answer is 'no' to either of these, suggest a couple more. 'What about Friday all day or Monday 9.30 a.m. – any good?' If the answer is still 'no', that's your chance to pass the ball to your contact. 'OK, if those are no good, just tell me your free slots over the next week or so and I'll fit in around you.'

If your contact is unwilling to give you any dates, you know that they are not interested enough in you or your proposition at this stage – or that they genuinely are too busy, in which case shoot for a date in the medium term.

Now here's where the real professional's experience comes in. Make sure that you get your contact's verbal confirmation of the date and time you just agreed. 'So, I'll see you at your offices at 10 a.m. on Wednesday 30th, OK?'

If there is sufficient time between your call and the meeting, drop them a line or email thanking them for the discussion, picking up any relevant points (possibly sending advance material if appropriate) and stating again how much you are looking forward to meeting them at the appointed date and time.

Nearer the meeting date, if your contact has a PA or secretary, check with them that the meeting is still in the diary. Be careful here, though – if you call your contact direct they may see it as an opportunity to cancel you if something more important has cropped up. Your purpose in checking with your contact's secretary is to avoid wasting your time, not to endanger the meeting.

When you are calling your contact's PA/secretary, remember to build rapport – they are critical to your success and you'll have a much better chance of keeping the meeting if they have enjoyed your conversation.

The jackpot could be a call away

While not every connector will be operating in the telephone sales arena, those who do will recognise the sinking feeling in the pit of their stomach after a series of rejections.

American sales guru Tom Hopkins has the best advice for creating the right frame of mind for cold calling. He says, 'Think of it as a slot machine – eventually it will pay off. Every one of your calls brings you closer to the right person and the right opportunity.'

If you're working on the basis of not knowing the name of the person you wish to telephone at an organisation, try this top tip from Tom. Phone and ask the receptionist who is responsible for whatever job title/function is your most likely contact. Once you have the name, ask them to spell it if needed – don't assume you know – ask them to pronounce it again if necessary so that you know the correct inflection. Finally, thank the receptionist profusely and say that their help is really appreciated – which it is!

The receptionist will put you through and, while the increasing trend is for senior people to answer their own phones nowadays, the likelihood is that you will reach a secretary/PA. The idea is to enlist their support, not to weasel round them!

The key here is to be as friendly as possible. Explain in a nutshell how you may be able to help their organisation and ask what the procedure is for meeting or speaking with the decision-maker you identified with the receptionist earlier. With a bit of luck they'll tell you the best way to do it. Capture their name for your records and say that you are really grateful for their help.

If, for whatever reason, their suggested approach doesn't work for you, go back to them, tell them that you've followed their advice without success and ask for further ideas. No one likes to feel that they don't have some power and influence to get things done – particularly for someone who has come over as friendly, professional and interested in them and their business.

Relax and go with the flow

The knack of telephone success is to stay in control of your emotions, so the sensible approach is to find a way to relax. And relax you must, because the doctors tell us that tension in your body makes your voice sound more shrill, strident, dull or lifeless – none of which are exactly the hallmarks of a breezy connector who has something good to say. So take a leaf out of the telephone professionals' book and learn how to relax quickly and unobtrusively while still sitting at your desk.

TRY THIS

No strange yoga positions here, just a simple and straightforward calming exercise. Here goes …

While seated, deliberately tighten your muscles. Really go to town. Clench your fists, curl up those toes, tighten your chest and take a deep breath. I guarantee you will feel tense. Hold that feeling for at least seven seconds. Now, slowly exhale and as you allow the air to escape from your body, feel the tension go with it. Let those fingers and toes go loose and generally let your body go as limp as a wet rag.

Take another deep breath and hold it for a count of five. This time when you let the air out make sure your jaw is as loose as can be. Imagine that it is swinging on a well-oiled ball joint. Now breathe quietly for ten seconds and allow that feeling of calmness and control (you *will* feel it) to spread throughout your body. Feel it going right into your fingertips and toes. Now add the icing on the cake. Clear your mind and see yourself rocking gently to and fro in a hammock on a sunny day as you gently sip a cool drink of your choice…

There, that's better… Now dial that number!

Another tip for those who spend most of their working life on the telephone is to take a few minutes out regularly to do a shortened version of this quick relaxation routine. You know how tense you can get very quickly holding a phone to your ear, hunching your shoulders, leaning over the desk and generally creating tension in your head, neck, shoulders and back. Give yourself a regular break, walk around, hang loose and you'll really feel the benefit in your mind, body and voice.

Picture the person

Imagine the person you are calling is sitting right opposite you. Speak to them directly and see them smiling and relaxed as you are dialling the number and introducing yourself. Telemarketers often place a photograph of their favourite person (often a boyfriend or girlfriend, spouse or other family member) on the desk in front of them and talk to the photograph. It's not as strange as it may seem and it definitely relaxes the voice because of the familiarity of the subject. It's amazing how quickly you'll forget who you're really talking to. Other telemarketing professionals prefer to use their imagination to create a 'picture' of the person they are talking to based on the sound of their voice and the way they speak. Try this one too, it's good fun!

Dial a smile

You've probably heard it before, but smiling as you make a call (and during it) creates a totally different voice sound – and mood – than keeping your mouth tightly shut. Try it a few times and you'll be convinced. It's hard to be 'down in the mouth' when you are smiling and while it's impossible to maintain a wide grin throughout the conversation, you can keep that smiley feeling throughout and sound optimistic, intelligent and enthusiastic. These are exactly the traits that give your listener the warm feeling you are after.

While you're at it, slow down. No doubt you have occasionally taken a phone call from someone who spoke extremely fast, either because they were nervous or because that's the way they normally converse. Either way, you would have found it difficult to keep up with the sense of what they were saying and would have felt that they lacked confidence, sincerity or persuasiveness. It *is* hard to persuade someone if they can't understand what you are saying! So the message is: slow down, take your time, articulate clearly and emphasise important words.

TRY THIS

If you're not sure how you come across on the phone, be brave and take this little test.

Get hold of a dictating machine and tape record your voice either speaking on the telephone or reading a passage from a book. If you aren't used to hearing the sound of your own voice played back to you, you will probably feel that you sound awful – that's just simply a function of hearing your voice as others hear it rather than as it resonates in your head when you are speaking.

Once you have got over the shock, listen again. Could your voice be warmer? Have another go and try to get some warmth in to it... Experiment a little and you'll soon find a much more lively and pleasant voice there on the tape.

Could you sound clearer? Again, a bit of practice with your dictating machine will soon have you sounding much clearer and you'll find yourself increasingly comfortable with the sound of your own voice.

Bring in enthusiasm as your background 'beat'

Be guided by what you hear and, where appropriate, copy the pace and tone of others who you feel really get their message and personality across on the telephone. It's not difficult, it's simply a question of observing what you do, building on your strengths and minimising some of those weaknesses you may have discovered during your tape-recorder exercise.

Remember to get 'enthusiasm' as the background beat to everything you say and you'll be well on the way to being a superb telephone connector.

Getting Your Ideas Across

Now that you have controlled your voice, you need to direct the conversation. Here's how the pros do it. First, and most important, they know exactly what they want to achieve from the call before their finger hits the dial. They've got all the information they need right beside them, including relevant background details on their contact. (It sounds obvious but we have all been in the position where we've not got a vital piece of information with us when we make a call ... and out of the window goes our professionalism, closely followed by our credibility.)

Be sure they know who you are

Assuming the pro has got through to their contact, they *always* introduce themselves ('Hello, it's Jane Brown from XYZ Company' or 'It's Jane' if the contact is well known to them). Don't, whatever you do, say 'Hi, it's me.' More often than not the person on the other end will be rifling through their contact book trying to match the voice to the person – and it's not a great way to build rapport if, after a pause, the other person says, 'Who is it?'

Get their attention straight away

A babbling brook is attractive, a babbling person is not. So get to the point after your introductory pleasantries. Highlight the benefits of your idea, offer, product or service (rather than trying to sell it) and instil in the other person a desire to talk to you further. Ultimately this means encouraging them to take action, usually to talk to you further on the telephone or in person. The ace connector knows never to leave the scene of a telephone conversation without agreeing a next action.

The secret of getting on an even footing

If you are serious about building a business partnership with your telephone contact you must be prepared for a rapport-building encounter between professionals of equal business stature. This doesn't mean you have to mislead your contact into thinking that you or your organisation are more successful than you are; it does mean that you should come over as a knowledgeable business person with credibility. That involves developing a compelling, attention-grabbing opening that will pique your listener's curiosity. It's curiosity that makes contacts want to know more about what you have to offer. If this sounds like a tall order, don't worry, it's not if you know how.

The trick is to focus on the measurable benefits of what you are offering and provide a 'hook' to get your contact into conversation mode, not to get them to listen to your 20-second 'pitch'.

IN PRACTICE

In 'shorthand' the archetypal persuasive connector's call would look something like this:

Greeting 'Good morning/afternoon, Mr.../Mrs.../John.'

Introduction Introduce yourself, your company, what you do ... and why it is relevant to the other person.

Thanks 'I appreciate you taking this call...'

Purpose Ask a question to pique their curiosity: 'If I could I show you how ...?' 'Would you be interested in exploring how this could help you?' (Explain the major benefit of your product/service and how it has worked for others.) If the answer is positive, paraphrase it and propose a meeting. 'Sell' them on the appointment/chat/discussion over coffee, not the idea or product.

Meeting 'Would Wednesday 3.30 p.m. in London be good, or how about 4.30 p.m. on Friday?'

Thanks Restate the agreed time and place, just to be sure they have it: 'OK, 4.30 p.m. Friday in London it is.' Send a confirmation note saying how nice it was to speak to them and that you are looking forward to seeing them.

Using the Technology Effectively

The explosion in telecommunications has meant that executives receive more calls than ever before. At the same time, thanks to personal computers, the need for administrative support in the form of secretaries has diminished considerably. Secretaries used to perform a valuable job in screening unwanted calls. Nowadays people resort to activating their voicemail or call answering system rather than be subjected to unwanted or untimely calls from people they don't know. 'Oh no, it's voicemail!' is a frustrated cry increasingly heard around the business world. You can often return to the office after a day's meetings and have 20 or more voice messages. Some may be from bosses and colleagues, others (maybe yours) will be from callers outside the organisation.

At one time it was business courtesy to return calls, and best practice was to return them by the end of the day. Unfortunately, the realities of business life now mean that the poor executive who replied to all the messages would get home just before midnight. Of course they don't do that. They choose the ones to respond to and ignore the rest. If you don't believe it, ask any salesperson how many returned calls they receive. How do *you* get onto the call-back list? Try this:

Use the answerphone/voicemail 'tease'

The secret is not to leave the traditional (boring) 'Hello, this is Nicola Barnett from Research Associates Inc. here. I wonder if you could call me back on 1234 when you have a moment? Many thanks.' Where's the incentive to return the call? Nicola has left bare facts, professionally sound but bland, especially when the poor executive may have many other messages like this.

The way to get someone to call you back is to treat voicemail messages like striptease – give a glimpse, but not too much. You don't have to be selling anything to use this technique, it works for social calls too. Here are a few 'teases' to get you into the swing of it:

- 'Bob, it's John here. I've just been talking to Ray about the project. He's got some news I know you'll find really interesting. Give me a call back on 4567 and I'll tell you more.'

- 'Mr Smith, it's Mark Wiggins here from XYZ Consultants. We've just finished an assignment with an organisation in your sector and saved them £2m on their purchasing arrangements. The same approach could work for you. Give me a call on 2345 when it's convenient and I'd be happy to tell you more.'

- 'John, Bob here. I've got the results of those lab tests we did – fascinating stuff. Call me when you have a minute.'

No doubt you've got the idea now and can think of appropriate teases for your friends, your colleagues and your contacts.

Be professional – even when you're not there

Top connectors change the message on their own voice-mail/answerphone every day because it shows professionalism and dynamism. We've all telephoned someone and been greeted by a two-month old message saying that they are on holiday. We've no need to debate what kind of image that leaves you with. Genuine oversight it may be, but it reflects badly.

Contrast that with a current message which says: 'Hi, this is Joanne Mattison. Thanks for calling. It's Wednesday 18th April, I'm in a meeting for most of the morning, but should be free and at my desk around 2 p.m. If you'd like to leave a message and your number now, please do so after the tone and I'll get back to you. Many thanks.'

Make it a habit to leave a message like this on your business voicemail either every evening before you leave the office or first thing in the morning. It needn't be long – or word perfect – the odd stumble is natural and often adds some 'personality' to it.

A word of caution, though: don't leave similar 'I'm out all day' messages on your home answerphone unless you want your house burgled!

IN PRACTICE

Interested to learn what their employees really feel, US food company The Pillsbury Company has set up a third-party voicemail system called In Touch which allows anyone to phone any time to give anonymous feedback. Transcripts of the calls go to senior management.

Have more than one conversation at a time

No, I'm not advocating making the best use of your time by having two phones pressed to your ear, I'm talking about conference calls, one of the best tools available to the networker. A conference call does exactly what its name suggests. You can have a 'conference' on the telephone with umpteen people joining in the discussion. The benefits to the connector are obvious: they can get their message across verbally to many people at once, get immediate feedback and interaction, and agree the way forward.

With telecommunications as they are nowadays, there's nothing to stop you having a conference call with people from all over the world. While there will never be a substitute for face-to-face interaction, think of the time and money saved by sitting in your office talking to all of your key colleagues around the world instead of jetting them all to some midpoint location to say the same thing.

Top connectors have developed the art of chairing such meetings so that everyone knows what's going on, who is speaking and the key aspects for discussion. Normally, the disciplines imposed mean that many participants in conference calls feel that they have had a more effective use of time than a face-to-face meeting with the same agenda.

IN PRACTICE

Most telecom providers offer a 'teleconference' facility where participants are given a central number to call and the call is administered by a trained 'host' who ensures that all participants are plugged into the discussions.

The cost is minimal compared with the very real business benefits. You may, of course, want to go a stage further and host a 'video conference'. As the name suggests, a video conference is one where the participants can see each other on a TV screen. You'll need to go to a special facility, but there are increasing numbers of them around. The benefits are arguably even greater than those of the phone-based conference call because you can see your fellow participants – and it is very important, as we know, to pick up body language and general demeanour, which can be masked in a telephone conference call situation.

CHAPTER 10

Connecting in Writing

MANY WOULD-BE CONNECTORS have never been formally taught how to write material intended to inform and persuade. And anyone who has been involved in the production of such material, whether it is a letter, memo or a formal proposal, knows that structuring the words is not always easy. However, the difference between a good and an average piece of prose can be the difference between winning and losing an opportunity or assignment. This chapter will help you to develop the skills of the professional writer and make you far more likely to achieve the results you want from your written communication.

The best piece of advice to begin with is that the more thinking you do at the start of the writing process, the less work you will have to do later. Your most important initial action is to think about what you want to say and why.

TRY THIS

Ask yourself these questions when you next sit down to write:

- Who is going to read what I've written?

- What is their level of knowledge and interest in me, my organisation and what we offer?

- What aspects do they particularly want information on?

- What do I *not* need to cover in my writing?

The answer to the last question is particularly relevant, as it is easy to fall into the trap of writing a great deal of irrelevant 'guff' and, as a result, cloud the persuasiveness of the rest of the document.

Like a great story, a good piece of writing should keep its reader's attention and lead them smoothly from one point to the next. Readability is crucial to your success. You will be competing for your reader's attention, so the more interesting and well written your work is, the more likely key decision-makers are to read it – and the better disposed they will be towards you.

Whatever form your writing takes it should:

1. Show the reader that you are on their side.

2. Lead them to your way of thinking through emphasising the benefits of your approach.

Showing the reader that you are on their side means writing from their point of view and demonstrating that you understand them. Once you have built a platform for your credibility by identifying with their situation, you can then move into persuading them that you or your organisation is their best option.

Writing Style

Whether you are writing a letter, a report, an email or a full-blown proposal document, the basic principles of connecting still hold fast. First, limit the points you want to make and pick the best – the ones of greatest importance to your readers.

The top connector's aim is to make sure that their key messages stand out, so their document conveys these even if it is only quickly scanned by their contact. This means, for example, putting your points in the order of importance to your reader.

This shows that you know what is a priority for them. Unlike the wedding at Cana, don't leave your best points until last. Some of your contacts will have the attention span of a flea (or simply have no time) and won't get to your crescendo of a finishing point.

Mind Your Language!

There is no need to try to impress with long words or complex sentences. An approach that uses everyday English and the first and second person, 'I', 'we', 'you', is far more powerful. Do as the great copywriters do and use the words you use in everyday language. A writing style which uses five-syllable words won't make you seem more intelligent, it will just frustrate your reader and put a barrier between them and you. When you edit your writing, imagine yourself speaking the words out loud.

A friendly rather than too formal style will be one that is likely to suit the vast majority of readers, but be careful of over-familiarity. Top connectors are approachable yet professional, and this should come over loud and clear in your writing style. Avoid unnecessary formality, for example:

Avoid	Use	Avoid	Use
Commence	Begin/Start	Accordingly	So
Terminate	End	In view of the fact that	Because
Utilisation	Use	Materialise	Happen/Occur
Despite the fact that	Although	Obtain	Get
Anticipate	Expect	Proceed	Go

Avoid unnecessary words or phrases, for example:

Avoid	Use	Avoid	Use
Connected together	Connected	Meet with	Meet
In close proximity	Near/Close	Fully expect	Expect
Period of time	Period	Decide upon	Decide

Watch out for adverbs too. They usually weaken the words associated with them and often add nothing. Use words like these with care:

Absolutely	Relatively	Substantially	Appreciably
Significantly	Considerably	Unduly	Virtually

Trawl your writing for clichés or jargon. Clichés are worn-out phrases or sentences. What presumably carried some impact when it was first coined can quickly become stale and hackneyed. Using jargon can be a good or a bad thing. It can save you and the reader some time if you use jargon you both understand and it can also bolster your credibility if you use some jargon of the reader's industry or even of the company you are writing to. But consider:

- Who else might read your document? Will they understand your language?

- Is the jargon, although familiar, really meaningful or just there to show you're 'part of the club'?

- Has any of your own jargon crept in? You may be so familiar with such phrases that you fail to notice them. Think 'reader' when you edit.

Turning on the Persuasion and Passion

Think of persuasion as moving someone from where they are now to where you want them to be – for example, to believe in what you are saying, to accept that you can meet their needs (for example in a competitive bid) or to realise they have come to a wrong conclusion about their needs.

The connector can do several things to move their readers.

Structure each point properly

Do as the top business writers do:

- **Identify the situation** Summarising the present problem, opportunity, complications or questions to be answered helps you to appear authoritative and understanding – just the image you want.

- **Explain how you can help** and why it should be you. Setting out the options and evaluation criteria positions you in relation to others.

- **Provide the proof** Show them the hard evidence that you can deliver on your promises.

- **Highlight the benefits** What's in it for them and why should they do what you want them to do? What difference will it make to them? When you've highlighted the benefits, go back and give them the 'So what?' test. Ask yourself if 'So what?' is likely to be your contact's reaction to each benefit you give. If so, strengthen your argument by making each benefit more relevant and tangible to them.

IN PRACTICE

Within its new product development project teams, Toyota has standardised written reports.

- All reports are written on one side of A4 paper.

- All reports follow the same format so that everyone knows where to find the definition of the problem, the responsible engineer and department, the result of the analysis and the recommendations. The standard format also helps the writer to make sure they have covered the important angles.

This short and sharp approach results in a clear statement of a problem and solutions.

Such clarity is not easy to attain, so the company gives engineers formal training in how to boil down what they want to communicate.

Make it eye-catching

Once you have written your words, make sure that all your hard work is translated into a layout that is designed to impress your reader. The way it looks will have a major impact on the decision-maker's impression of your competence. First impressions are often last impressions, and your written communication could end up in the wastebasket before a word is read if you let yourself down with poor layout and presentation.

A picture speaks a thousand words, so they say, so if your document is becoming long, look for chances to replace text with a diagram or a chart. Good graphics can communicate information more easily, and interestingly, to a reader.

Develop eye-catching headings or titles that reflect your key messages.

Sometimes in formal tender situations the approach to be taken is stipulated, for example: 'Your tender submission must be no more than 30 pages long and consist of . . .' But even in these circumstances a well-structured and written document in a pleasing typeface will stand out from the crowd.

If it's appropriate, get some colour in there too. That's not to say you should make your document look like a rainbow, but picking out the headlines and subheads in a different colour is classy, as is producing any diagrams, photographs or other visual material. With modern computer technology all of these can be done without fuss.

Use logic and levers

A persuasive piece of writing needs to be based on facts and logic as well as being well-structured and easy to follow. Illogical or downright inaccurate reasoning won't persuade anyone. The most common error in writing, say the experts, is logic jumps, where one step (or more) in the reasoning is left out. It's that missing step that destroys the persuasive flow. You may not spot it, but the chances are it will spring out at the reader. So get someone objective to read your material before you fire it off.

But logic on its own is not necessarily persuasive. To be persuaded your reader must:

- See problems with their present position which are worth solving, or see opportunities worth grasping.

- See that beneficial change is possible.

- Believe that you and your ideas are credible and worth any risks and costs involved.

- Believe that your approach is better than the others available.

Connectors use those problems, opportunities and benefits as positive or negative 'levers' to move the readers towards what they want to happen. Let's have a closer look at these.

- **Positive levers** are what a reader has told you they want; the benefits they will gain from adopting your proposal, the pay-off for going ahead. In the business context they might be cost reduction, increased production, better-quality recruits or improved margins.

- **Negative levers** are the costs of the reader's existing position; for example the inability to expand a computer system, shrinking margins, excessive labour costs or slower product development than the competition. They might also be the costs of not adopting your proposed approach, for example losing ground on the competition or missing a market opportunity.

And there you have it, the keys to successful written communication. You see it every day – not necessarily in the letters you receive or reports you read, but you will see it in the quality newspapers. Many of the techniques highlighted here are those used by quality journalists who have to get a factual message across in an interesting way in as few words as possible. Emulate their style and you won't go too far wrong in your business or social writing.

THE CONNECTOR'S TOOLKIT

Write like a quality journalist with this ten-point action plan:

1. **Grab your reader** Messages unseen are messages unreceived. If your key points are submerged in fine print, they neither persuade nor have the sense of urgency or conviction you need.

2. **Make your arguments evident** That means they must be simple, repeated, short and to the point.

3. **Write headlines that demand attention** Five times as many people read headlines in advertisements as read the text underneath. Like all good advertising copywriters, get your promise, claim and main point into the headline and reaffirm them in your opening paragraph.

4. **Use subheadings liberally** Subheads break up text and summarise the main issue of the next section. Cross-heads, as journalists call them, create curiosity and are carriers of your key points. If you don't believe their power, just look at any newspaper – they all use them.

5. **Use bullet points and numbers,** especially when listing several disparate points on a range of issues. Bullets corral them together nicely and give structure where there is none.

6. **Use 'concrete' words** rather than abstract ones and avoid jargon like the plague, unless you are absolutely sure your readers will know what it means.

7. **Write 'actively'** Active writing is more direct and forceful, uses fewer words, conveys energy and is more likely to conjure up a picture. For example 'The building was destroyed by the storm' is weaker than 'The storm destroyed the building.'

8. **Check and check again** Errors in typing, spelling, numbers and grammar rightly or wrongly shout that the author is a sloppy thinker. A careless attitude towards small issues portrays a careless attitude towards bigger matters and tarnishes what could be brilliant work. Get someone else to look over your work and make sure that you use the computer's spell and grammar checker. No one has an excuse for poor grammar these days.

9. **Watch your face and appearance** Writing at length in CAPITALS or *italics* makes for harder reading. If you are using a small point size (below 10), you'd better send a magnifying glass as well. Very few people feel comfortable reading small print. Make your writing easy on the eye and also ensure that the typeface you use reflects the nature of your organisation and your message.

10. **Be clear and brief** Take the advice of the Plain English Campaign and keep your sentence length to 15–20 words, lines between 7 and 23 words, and use everyday English.

Whatever form your communication takes, it *can* stand out from the crowd if you follow these guidelines. Connectors recognise the importance of producing lively, interesting yet professional written material. Give yourself the best chance of getting your message across by doing the same.

Using the 'Net' to Connect

I N TODAY'S FAST-PACED world, electronic means of getting and keeping in touch have become a major part of doing business. Fifteen years ago the thought that email could be a top connector's most powerful weapon would have been laughable. But thanks to Microsoft and chums, all that's changed.

Now, as we all know, it's possible to communicate with almost anyone in the world, almost anywhere and almost instantaneously, through the Internet. And therein lies the problem for the connector – how to focus this very potent communication tool on the right targets to get the right results. Email has become a welcome addition to the connector's written communication armoury. But those in the know recognise that it must be treated with respect.

It's fantastic to be able to send a quick message over the ether to contacts and have them respond within seconds. It's less intrusive than a telephone call, as a message can be read at a time which suits the recipient. And, of course, it has the great advantage of being able to carry all sorts of document attachments, links to websites and fancy graphics with it. This chapter is not about the latest gizmos to trawl the web or search for contacts; there are plenty of books that cover these areas. Instead it's a look at the connector's approach to communicating electronically.

The Special Techniques of Email Relationships

As always there's a right and a wrong way to go about things. Take email style, for example. The accepted protocol of emails is that they can be more informal than letters or memos. Email is an ideal medium for a quick note, a short comment or request for information – but watch out, because emails are just as legally binding as a carefully checked letter or memo, and are very easily forwarded to as many people as the recipient wishes, often by doing no more than typing an address and pressing a button.

When sending an email it always pays to check what you are saying and ask yourself whether you would still feel comfortable with your message if it were forwarded to others. At the same time check your spelling. Not all of us are trained typists and horrible *faux pas* occur as a result. It may only be a quick note, but a silly grammatical error can have the effect of considerably diminishing your reputation in the eyes of your contact.

Your quickly dashed off note may actually tell your contact that:

- You can't spell.

- You can't type.

- You can't be bothered to get it right.

- You don't know how to use the spell checker on your machine.

Treat email as you would a formal letter. Are you in the habit of sending letters littered with mistakes? I doubt it.

IN PRACTICE

If you are attaching any information, make absolutely sure that it is the right document or attachment before firing it off. Open the document to check. Too many times people have inadvertently attached a similarly named document to an email to me – some of these documents were definitely not for my eyes.

The electronic wizardry of email is a powerful tool, but don't let your own carelessness cause it to backfire.

That's a warning on what not to do, but what do the best connectors do in this area? Here are some practical tricks of the trade to build your relationships over the web.

Be an email address collector

Naturally, connectors gather email addresses for their contacts. Usually the address will be on their business cards, but if not, they'll ask for it. Why? Because many connectors are increasingly recognising the value of email as a time-saving mechanism for keeping in touch. They'll obviously use email (if it's the most appropriate method) to say 'It was good to meet, look forward to seeing you again' and they'll put a read receipt on it to tell them when their new contact has actually opened and read their message. They'll then know when it's the most appropriate time to make that follow-up call.

For your eyes only

The smartest connectors have also discovered the value of the 'blind cc' (copy correspondence) address line on the email header.

Using this 'blind cc' line they can input dozens of individual email addresses or 'group codes' and send a message that will appear as if it had gone to only one recipient. That is, each person who opens the email only sees themselves as the receiver of the message.

This is a critical time-saver for connectors in sales or business development, for example, who want to reach a group with an idea, an offer, an invitation or similar standard message.

The key to success in using 'blind cc' effectively is in the construction of the email message. This is one example that's been used to invite clients to a specific industry event.

From: Tony Southam
To: jameshalsall@halsall.co.uk
Subject: Global Retail Forum 24 September

We're inviting selected clients in the retail sector to a special day-long retail forum at the Hilton in London on 24 September.

The day will be chaired by Jan Hackner, a senior vice president of Wal-Mart, and will focus on how the key world retail players are gaining competitive advantage.

Our own EPOS specialists will also be sharing their latest research on buyer trends and we'll be having a senior retail CEO as a guest speaker.

I thought I'd alert you to this opportunity early so that you could put the date in your diary. Let me know if you wish to attend or need more information. Simply reply to me to register your place. I'll send further details to you.

Regards

Tony

As the information in the email is the same for everyone and as everyone on his list is a client in the retail sector, Tony can send the 'nearly personalised' email above in a matter of seconds. No expensive postage, no stuffing of envelopes. Equally importantly, Tony's key contact recipients can read this message in a minute, decide whether or not they would like to attend, press the button and, hey presto, Tony very quickly knows who can and can't make the event. He can then follow up specific queries and if necessary send a tailored reminder to those who have not yet responded. It's a quick, efficient and 'almost personalised' way to connect with many people with the same common interest.

You're in very good company

Conversely, sending a message to a group of people where all of the names feature in your email header is also a technique of the champions. This way you can create the feel of a high-level élitist group by having a small number of people – the names of each of which are known and respected by the others – on your distribution list. So, a development of Tony's previous note may read:

> To:
> Chairman@marksandspencer
> Ceo@maceys
> Chairman@next
> Ceo@thomascook
> Chairman@boots
>
> From: Tony Southam
> Subject: Retail Chairman/CEO dinner 24 September
>
> Many thanks for responding to my previous note. Delighted you are able to attend the Forum on 24 September. We have been fortunate enough to secure the presence of [guest speaker] for a discussion over dinner of the key issues affecting retail businesses today.
>
> It promises to be a thought-provoking and stimulating discussion among peers, and I do hope your diary will allow you to join us for dinner following the Forum. Please feel free to reply directly to this note, or alternatively have your secretary call me on [tel. no].
>
> Yours
>
> Tony

Open me up!

Another essential top tip from the electronic connectors is based on the advertising copywriter's skills. They use the 'subject' line on the email header to intrigue, beguile, amuse, generally arouse curiosity and grab the attention of the reader.

Why? Because many people, especially those in large organisations, receive dozens of emails every day. They prioritise those they will read first and leave others until they have some time – possibly sometime never?

The secret of getting onto someone's 'to read' list, especially if they don't know you, is to use the subject line for your 'headline', just as an advertising copywriter does to catch your eye in a magazine. Clearly this will depend on your subject matter, but the trick is not to give too much detail in the header, otherwise why would the recipient open your email in the first place?

You might want to tease with headers such as:

- This has just worked for your competitor ...

- Do you know the three big issues in your sector?

- Important news just in ...

- Would you have done this ...?

- [Leading figure in the sector] warns ...

- Does this affect you?

- How would you feel about a 20 per cent reduction in cost [or whatever benefit you offer]?

- You need to act fast to ...

- The latest survey findings showed ...

But a word of warning – don't use these too often, especially not the same header with the same person, and make sure that your headline does relate to what you are saying in your email. No one likes to be duped into reading messages under false pretences and it won't do your reputation or credibility any good if the recipient feels that you've manipulated them. So act like the champion connectors and give some real thought to making your email sound interesting and relevant in your subject headline.

What's news with you?

Connectors are cottoning on to the business benefits of the e-newsletter. You may have seen an annual electronic letter sent, for example, at Christmas by families to all of their far-flung friends and relatives telling them the highlights of the last 12 months. These have quickly become a very popular and easy way to produce an update incorporating anything from basic text through to complex graphics and pictures.

Now connectors are adapting the approach for business to keep their network of contacts up to speed with what they've been doing and with whom. The e-newsletter is great for freelancers, contract workers, interim managers and others who rely on a known and established network of contacts for work.

A quick update to an already created distribution list could be just the right thing at the right time, especially if you've been working in a new area of the sector, or one that's particularly current or successful.

Best practice means that you don't overblow your own trumpet – nobody welcomes a strident 'sell' – but most recipients with whom you already have a relationship would be interested in a quick update once in a while. Simply use your finishing remarks to invite any of your contacts to call you or respond to your email if they want to know more.

Connectors are using the e-newsletter concept to share new ideas they've been working on with non-conflicting clients as a soft-sell way to generate interest from others. Here's an example:

> We've just finished working on a project with a client in the construction sector where we've managed to cut their purchasing costs by 20 per cent by identifying efficiencies and consolidating their supplier base. This is similar to savings we've made for others in the industrial products and retail sectors, so the chances are that the approach may work in yours too.

If you want to find out more, just give me a call, or reply to this note.

All the best

Frances

There's no hard sell in the note above – the author is simply sharing what's been achieved for others and inviting the recipients to consider whether this is an area they would wish to find out more about. It works, but only because it is relevant to Frances' contacts and their business.

Intranets

Many organisations have their own intranets, a closed community of employees who can send messages to each other electronically. This means that the aspiring connector can, in most instances, communicate with the entire workforce with little difficulty. While for most a broadcast of this nature is likely to be very rare (unless you are the CEO or chief communications officer), it does mean that you can easily set up email addresses for specific groups of people you would want to communicate with on a regular basis.

In the old days, sending a hard copy (paper) memo to a large group of people was a mammoth administrative task. Now the connector can send the electronic equivalent in seconds. By being proactive in circulating relevant information of genuine interest and value to others you can very quickly become the hub of the communications channel on your chosen areas of interest.

Websites

If you are self-employed, run a business and need to promote your services you'll probably already have considered the value of having a website. While the initial fever of website development has diminished somewhat as people take a more realistic view of who is likely to visit their site, there is no doubt that for some connectors a website adds credibility to their offer.

You can build a simple website very quickly with minimum fuss, but think also about the image you are trying to convey. People will ultimately be looking at your site and making judgements about you as a result of what they see. The litmus test is this: is your site one a top connector would be proud to be associated with?

And don't just build it and forget it. When you construct a site you also implicitly commit to invest time in updating it regularly. Reading patently dated material brings you down several rungs on the connector's ladder. It will appear that you are either out of touch or not bothered. Neither of these labels will help you to connect effectively over the Net.

Interest Groups and Chat Rooms

For some connectors a great source of finding like-minded people are the Internet's interest groups and 'chat rooms'. Why not explore those relevant to your industry, profession and passions? Beware, though, of providing your email and other details to others unless you specifically want them to contact you.

The idea is that you have the capability to connect proactively with those contacts and facilities you find valuable, not to be bombarded with messages and more from people you don't know and don't have the opportunity to check out on a face-to-face basis.

Be a Good 'Net' Citizen

Sending emails wantonly to any person or organisation with an email address, 'spamming' as it is known, is both an offence and offensive. It wastes valuable time and resources, so don't do it. Connectors wouldn't.

THE CONNECTOR'S TOOLKIT

The checklist below was provided by Internet communication guru Guy Levine. He runs courses for business people in how best to use the Net to network and market themselves. He says that most people using the Net are like beginner drivers – they've only just got a handle on the fundamentals. With a few 'advanced' lessons he transforms their performance.

Try these tips for starters:

- Emails have an informality about them. They are read quickly and often discarded quickly. Therefore, keep your messages as short as possible. Write them as if you were leaving some-body a note. Don't write in capital letters – this is SHOUTING in email language.

- Send emails that will stand out from the crowd and deliver a powerful marketing message. How many plain, boring emails do you get? Most email programs are now able to read html/rich text emails. This means that you can change the colour of text, add graphics and change the fonts of the text. Watch out, though, if you use a font on your computer and it's not on the other person's, as it will show up differently.

- Make sure that every email that goes out includes your con-tact details at the bottom and, more importantly, what you do! This acts as branding, just as your logo does on your let-terhead. If you want to think out of the box, put the details at the top of the email, so that people have to read them!

- Use the computer's address book to manage your contacts and send multiple emails. Your address book should be your prized possession. If you have lots of contacts, don't forget to back it up, so that if a system crash comes, you still have your addresses.

- Learn how to send messages to groups of people such as clients, new leads and personal contacts to keep you at the forefront of your contacts' minds. Use Groups to split contacts into their different categories – suppliers, contacts and customers, for example. Once you have done this, you will be able to send them emails by only entering one address. 'Top of mind' marketing works by sending a message to people regularly. How many messages will you have to send to prospective customers for them to remember to buy from you or recommend you to someone who will?

- If you make the step to using email as a major marketing and communication tool, make sure you keep all your emails organised. Use folders to separate the messages into groups of similar subject and save time by not having to look through hundreds of emails to find what you want.

- Learn the quick way to find information from a large amount of emails. Instead of searching frustratedly for emails, use the 'Find' option in your email program. Click 'Find' and enter the person's name or email address and you will be given a list of all the messages that person has sent to you. Couldn't be much easier, could it?

- Save your important emails in case of a system crash or for use in other documents. If your system crashes and you don't have paper copies or a backup, all your information may be lost. Make backing up a regular habit.

Appendix: the End ... or Just the Beginning?

So now we've seen how the champion connectors do it. Maybe you've read the book from cover to cover, or perhaps you've just dived at random into sections that have attracted your attention. It doesn't really matter which, because you're here now and the next words you read are the most important of all: *just do it.*

Behind that glib advertising slogan is a powerful truth. Reading about how to connect effectively and understanding what makes for great networking won't do much for you unless you put some of the ideas into practice for yourself.

I'm not talking about slavishly applying each and every tip, but I'd be absolutely failing in my duty to you if I didn't use every ounce of my persuasiveness to encourage you to go out and meet the people you want to meet, and to use some of the hundreds of tips you'll find in here – the ones that suit *you* and your personality. Developing an attitude that helps you to put yourself in other people's shoes is the key to success.

Putting others first isn't woolly-headed thinking, a Pollyanna attitude or a statement loaded with religious undertones; it's sound business and relationship practice that generates positive results. Give people your time, attention and goodwill and you'll be repaid with massive interest by those you choose to connect with.

Sometimes, proactively making such connections will stretch your comfort zone – you may recognise that ill-at-ease feeling in the pit of your stomach and the almost imperceptible (but very real) little voice in your head that says: 'I can't possibly...' Treat these as networkers' growing pains, because they will pass.

Maybe one of the networker's skills highlighted in these pages is particularly important to you right now, in which case you have an obvious starting-point. If you don't feel the urge to concentrate on any one area, can I suggest that you flick back through the book and use the action plan template below to record those techniques you wish to build into your networking repertoire.

My Connecting Action Plan

My top ten actions

1. Action

Reassess my business cards.

What will I do specifically?

Include a photo and better description of the benefits of my service.

By when *Reprint by end Dec.*

2. Action

What will I do specifically?

By when

3. Action

What will I do specifically?

By when

4. Action

What will I do specifically?

By when

5. Action

What will I do specifically?

By when

6. Action

What will I do specifically?

By when

7. Action

What will I do specifically?

By when

8. Action

What will I do specifically?

By when

9. Action

What will I do specifically?

By when

10. Action

What will I do specifically?

By when

If you have set yourself some 'actions', your success as an ace connector now depends only on a couple of things: maintaining your enthusiasm for developing relevant new contacts and committing to apply the principles encapsulated in these pages. We're talking about taking small steps every day – steps like following up the new contact you made instead of forgetting about them, making the first move to introduce yourself to a stranger and experimenting with a voicemail 'tease' to see what response you get. Or how about practising a self-introduction until it trips effortlessly off your tongue, taking the initiative to reconnect with someone you've not spoken to in a while or trying different seating arrangements at meetings to see what level of rapport each gives? Why not use the presentation skills tips so that your next act of persuasion registers a '*Wow*, that's different!' on your audience's Richter Scale, use the meetings checklist to make the most of your next gathering or resolve to keep your contacts up to date with a regular email missive?

If you've read a fair chunk of this book, you'll know that the examples above are just some of the many actions great connectors take. Each has the potential to make a real difference to your networking. Choose those of most interest and value to you and you'll be much more likely to succeed.

What will you get out of all this effort – and where's the pay-back? How about more enjoyable interaction with people for one thing, better social and business relationships for another, and the satisfaction that comes from the knowledge that you are in a position to contribute to your network ... and what's more, you'll have a ball in the process!

As you discovered earlier in the book, you already have great connections and there's no better time than right now to tap into your network. So, just plunge in and, to change the advertising slogan a bit, 'Just *enjoy* doing it!'

Further Reading

Jay Abraham, *Getting Everything You Can Out of All You've Got*, Piatkus Books, 2000

Andrew and Faulkner, *NLP: The New Technology of Achievement*, Nicholas Brealey Publishing, 1996

Lillian Bjorseth, *Breakthrough Networking: Building Relationships That Last*, Duoforce Enterprises, 1996

Meribeth Bunch, *Creating Confidence: How to Develop your Personal Power and Presence*, Kogan Page, 1999

Philippa Davies, *Your Total Image: How to Communicate Success*, Piatkus Books, 1990

Ferguson, Dennis and Walker, *Creating New Clients: Marketing and Selling Professional Services*, Cassell, 1998

Fisher and Vilas, *Power Networking: 55 Secrets for Personal and Professional Success*, Mountain Harbour Publications, 1995

Thomas Freese, *Secrets of Question Based Selling*, Sourcebooks Inc., 2000

David Hall, *In the Company of Heroes: An Insider's Guide to Entrepreneurs at Work*, Kogan Page, 1999

Tom Hopkins, *Selling for Dummies*, IDG Books Worldwide, 1995

David Lewis, *Winning New Business: A Practical Guide to Successful Sales Presentations*, Piatkus Books, 1993

David Lewis, *The Secret Language of Success*, Corgi, 1990

John Lockett, *Powerful Networking*, Orion Business Books, 1999

Harry Lorraine, *How to Develop a Super Power Memory*, A. Thomas & Co., 1967

Leil Lowndes, *How to Talk to Anyone: 92 Little Tricks for Big Success in Relationships*, Thorsons, 1999

Harvey MacKay, *Swim with the Sharks Without Being Eaten Alive*, Warner, 1998

Newstrom and Scannell, *The Big Book of Team Building Games*, McGraw Hill, 1997

Anthony Parinello, *Selling to VITO (the Very Important Top Officer)*, Adams Media Corporation, 1999

Allan Pease, *Body Language: How to Read Others' Thoughts by Their Gestures*, Sheldon Press, 1997

David Peoples, *Selling to the Top*, Wiley, 1993

Susan Roane, *How to Work a Room: Learn the Strategies of Savvy Socialising – for Business and Personal Success*, Warner Books, 1988

Michael Roe, *Marketing Professional Services: Winning New Business in the Professional Services Sector*, Butterworth Heinemann, 1998

Morey Stettner, *The Art of Winning Conversation*, Prentice Hall, 1995

Kim Tasso, *Selling Skills for Professionals*, Hawksmere, 1999

John Timperley, *Barefoot on Broken Glass: The Five Secrets of Success in a Massively Changing Business World*, Capstone, 2000

Thanks also to Guy Levine at NMD UK for his tips on building email relationships. Contact him on www.nmduk.com. And to David Thomas, world memory champ. Contact him on info@davidthomas.tr

Thank you for giving this book your time and consideration. I really do appreciate it. And, in the true spirit of connecting, if you have any comments on the content, ways in which it can be improved or tips and techniques you have found valuable, feel free to email me at john.timperley@uk.pwcglobal.com I'd be delighted to hear from you.

Index

Note: page numbers in *italics* refer to diagrams

Other Business Titles Published by Piatkus Books

Alder, Harry, *Corporate Charisma*, 1999
Alder, Harry, *NLP for Managers*, 2000
Alder, Harry, *Train Your Brain*, 2000
Allen, David, *Getting Things Done*, 2002
Bennis, Warren, *Reinventing Leadership*, 1997
Breier, Mark, *The Ten Second Internet Manager*, 2000
Brondmo, Hans Peter, *The Engaged Customer*, 2002
Dertouzos, Michael, *What Will Be*, 1998
Edward Russo, J. & Schoemaker, J.H., *Winning Decisions*, 2002
Fullerton, Fiona, *How to Make Money from Your Property*, 2002
Godefroy, Christian, *The Complete Time Management System*, 1996
Green, Cynthia R., *Total Memory Workout*, 2001
Hill, Napoleon, *Napoleon Hill's Unlimited Success*, 2000
Hill, Napoleon, *Napoleon Hill's Keys to Success*, 2000
Hill, Napoleon, *Napoleon Hill's Positive Action Plan*, 2000
Jackson, Tom, *The Perfect CV*, 1997
James, Judi, *Bodytalk at Work*, 2001
Peppers, Don, *Enterprise One to One*, 1998
Peppers, Don, *The One to One Future*, 1996
Pont, Tony, *Interviewing Skills for Managers*, 1998
White, Alasdair, *Continuous Quality Improvement*, 1997
White, Alasdair, *The Essential Guide to Developing Your Staff*, 1999